PALESTINE

IN BLACK AND WHITE

This book is dedicated first to my mother for saving my drawings
when I was a child; my father, for taking me by the hand to my first
drawing competitions; my siblings, my greatest supporters; and to
Athar Hodali and dear Salma, for putting up with my absences both
while I was preparing this book and when I was in prison.

PALESTINE
IN BLACK AND WHITE

Mohammad Sabaaneh

SAQI

Published 2018 by Saqi Books
2

ISBN 978-0-86356-940-1

The EU GPSR authorised representative is Logos Europe, 9 rue Nicolas
Poussin, 17000 La Rochelle, France. Email: contact@logoseurope.eu

First published in Great Britain in 2018 by

Saqi Books
Gable House, 18-24 Turnham Green Terrace
London W4 1QP
www.saqibooks.com

Printed by PBtisk a.s.

CONTENTS

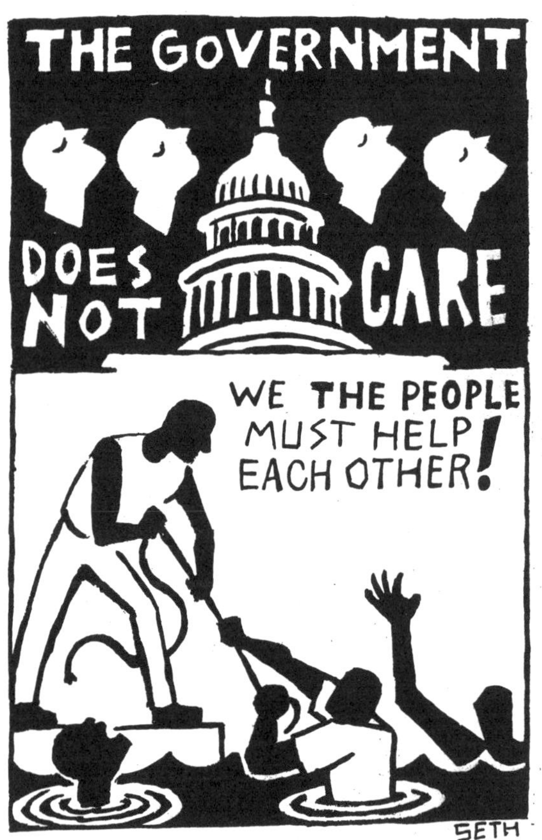

THE GOVERNMENT
DOES NOT CARE
WE THE PEOPLE MUST HELP EACH OTHER!
SETH

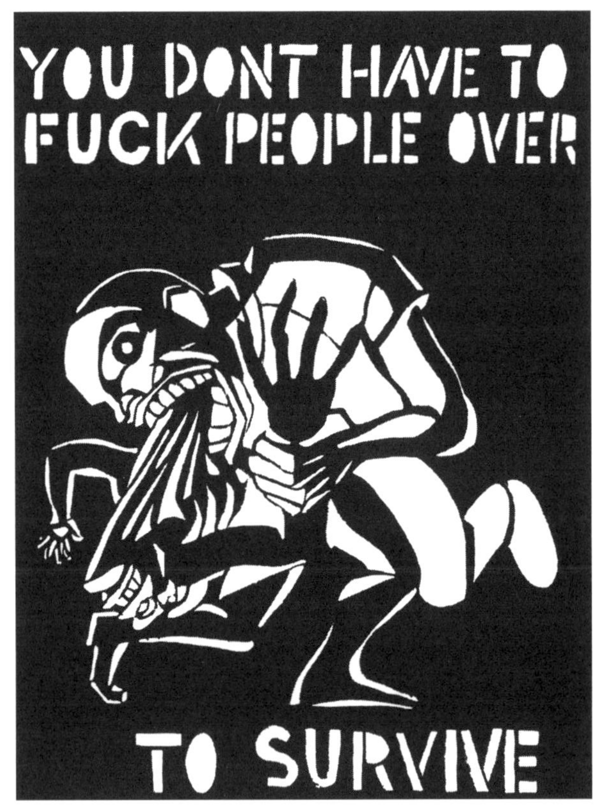

YOU DONT HAVE TO FUCK PEOPLE OVER
TO SURVIVE

SABAANEH'S SOCIAL SURREALISM

Foreword and Cartoons by Seth Tobocman

Can there be an accurate depiction of an insane situation? Why should we draw in perspective when the world has lost its perspective? When reality becomes bizarre, social realism gives way to social surrealism.

Mohammad Sabaaneh is a young Palestinian artist who joins a long tradition of Arab political cartoonists. For over a hundred years, the Arab countries have had newspapers in which the issues of the day are hotly debated. Such newspapers do not pretend to be neutral or polite. This is a partisan political press. These papers are often punctuated with illustrations. The intention of such drawings is not decorative but deeply didactic. It is the job of the cartoonist to explain complex political problems in such a way that the simplest person can understand them. The artist deploys an arsenal of well-understood symbols that speak to the history of the nation. He tries to combine them in new ways to describe a continually changing contemporary situation. But this is more than an intellectual exercise. This is a form of militant activism, and it has its risks.

Naji al-Ali, perhaps the most famous Palestinian cartoonist, was assassinated in 1987. His popular cartoons provide an accurate picture of Israel's persecution of the Palestinians, but he also called out corruption among Arab leaders, and so it has never been clear who was responsible for his execution. More recently, Syrian cartoonist Ali Ferzat had his hands broken by thugs for satirising President Assad. Ahmad Nady has been jailed over and over again for cartoons critical of successive Egyptian regimes. As the Egyptian military dictatorship consolidates power, more and more Egyptian cartoonists prefer to publish anonymously rather than risk arrest.

So it is not surprising at all that Mohammad Sabaaneh did some of his best artwork during the six months he was held in an Israeli prison, or that he has more recently received death threats for publishing an entirely positive portrait of the Prophet Mohammad.

When I look at the drawings of Mohammad Sabaaneh, I see the tortured, compressed, and crowded space that is everyday life for ordinary Palestinians. His cartoons capture this maze of walls, checkpoints, twenty-four-hour-a-day curfews, and prison cells punctuated by bombings, soldiers, tanks, and commonplace killings in a way that photojournalism fails to.

To describe this impossible landscape, Mohammad Sabaaneh draws on the language of twentieth-century cubism. The distortion of urban space of Braque and Picasso. But the modernists were not sure if the technological world would be a curse or a blessing. There was the geometric beauty of Picasso's nudes and still life paintings as well as the hysteria of his *Guernica*. Sabaaneh's drawings are closer to the *Guernica* for sure. But even the *Guernica* seems to explode outward into space while Mohammad's world implodes, trapped in the crammed frame. Mohammad shows us children inside a prison inside a city that grows from a tired man's back, and this tired man is also inside a prison. 'This,' Sabaaneh tells us, 'is Palestine!'

Even Sabaaneh's comic strips employ a pattern of painfully narrow panels, arranged like the spaces between prison bars. It is uncomfortable to view the world through this tiny slit. Mohammad never lets us forget where he is or how hard it is to be there.

It is hard to look at. It should be. This is angry art, ruthless and relentless. And who has more right to be angry than the children of Palestine? Born into a box, without the human and democratic rights many of us take for granted. This is the landscape that the West has created through almost a hundred years of political and military intervention. This is a man-made wilderness. A world we made, which reflects our own madness. In the words of Colin Powell, 'You broke it, you own it.' I am glad this collection is being published and made available to people around the world. Everyone needs to see these drawings.

INTRODUCTION

My first encounter with Palestine was through my mother's stories of Palestinian *fedayeen* (freedom fighters). Growing up in the Palestinian diaspora in Kuwait, I listened to her stories and constructed fantasy images of a Palestinian hero who struggled for freedom and justice in an idealised Palestine. During the summers, we would go to that idealised land for family visits, and years later when I recalled those visits, the big fig tree that my siblings and I used to play around seemed more luscious and green than any other tree. Other memories are not so benign; upon crossing the bridge from Jordan, I was aware even as a child that those in control were armed and spoke in a foreign language. I remember, too, crouching beneath a window in my grandparents' house where my grandmother hid us when the Israeli army stormed the neighbourhood, their helmets visible above the window sill. We returned to our homeland for good just before the second intifada (uprising) began in September 2000. My return enabled me to further develop the image of the Palestinian

hero who struggled against injustice, which found expression in my drawings time and time again.

The idea for this book began to take shape during the two weeks or so that I spent in solitary confinement in an Israeli occupation prison. Detained in 2013 for five months, my experience was not that different from that of thousands of other Palestinian detainees; less typical was my placement in solitary confinement following the end of interrogation. I had no idea how long my ordeal might last. I was being held in 'administrative detention,' a provision of the military laws that Israel has applied continuously since 1967 to the indigenous Palestinians of the West Bank and Gaza. Under these laws, which date back to the days of British rule, detention can be imposed for renewable six-month terms and is in theory indefinite. I spent the long hours thinking about creating a book that would depict all aspects of Palestinian life through snapshots of both the heroic and the ordinary, which like a mosaic becomes whole when one sees all the pieces together.

Like other detainees, I was shuttled from one prison to another and from one cell to another to accommodate the whims of my jailer. In detention, I got to know my heroes and witnessed their agonies; they longed for the banal details of ordinary lives, such as lighting a cigarette, conversing with a loved one, basking under the heat of the sun, or sipping a cup of coffee as they pleased and not as dictated by a set timetable.

I had drawn thousands of prisoner-heroes in the past, but in prison I felt completely impotent. Unable to portray myself as a hero, I surrendered to my weaknesses, for we all love, miss, fear and feel pain, and I had to confront the inescapable question: Was everything I drew a lie?

I tried to answer this question through sketches that I drew during the long periods in solitary detention. Through their artistic and literary efforts, the artists, writers, and intellectuals among us have always insisted that Palestinian prisoners are heroes, and prisoners themselves have been willing to adopt this view, I later learned, as a survival tactic to protect our souls from the dehumanising conditions in which we found ourselves and to safeguard our ability to resist. As a tactic, it was vital in keeping our spirits high.

Placing detainees in isolation was one method of interrogation and psychological torture used. To fight the isolation, I pretended I was a journalist whose mission it was to convey to the world at large what detention in an Israeli prison is like. During one of my interrogation sessions, I managed to steal some paper and a pencil, and then I listed some cartoon ideas, cramming as many ideas as I could on a single sheet. I hid the sheet of paper from my jailers until I was sent to prison, where I had access to more paper and pencils. I created sketches without any details that would convey that the subject matter was prison life because I was afraid that they might be confiscated. I drew things like the bus that transported prisoners from one facility to another; the transportation was a kind of torture too, because the bus was a metal contraption that was ice-cold in winter and stifling in summer, and transportation could take anywhere from three to seven days. I drew sick prisoners and prisoners who thought constantly about the daily activities of their children and about family visits. I smuggled rough sketches out with every prisoner who was released. When I was released,

I collected my sketches and completed the cartoons.

This book, I hope, presents a candid portrayal of Palestinian life to the wider world. My visualisation of the 'subject' includes not only Palestinians but also the occupier. I tried to expand my lens to spot the humanity of the occupier, but this effort proved difficult to sustain when an Israeli soldier placed handcuffs around my wrists, or dragged me to an interrogation room, or prevented me from moving from one part of my homeland to the other. With each violation, the occupier denied my humanity in order to justify his violence toward me. Consequently, I could not make the image of the occupier aesthetically pleasing, even when I acknowledge that in the process of exerting his political will, the occupier is also occupied.

In some of my sketches, occupier and occupied are hard to tell apart. I felt ugly when I was in my cell, and I still remember the reflection of my face on the jail truck as I was being transported and my attempt to recognise my features. I used my cell's rough walls to file my nails so I wouldn't look as degraded as the system was designed to make me feel. Ultimately, an awful reality cannot be prettified; our reality includes the bodies of children under the remains of homes bombed by Israeli military planes, and such realities are ugly.

The cartoons in this book are my attempt to tell the story of Palestine pictorially and to place it in a global context, and in so doing to cast light on the human dimension, all too often forgotten in political discussions.

While I was in prison, I lacked the instruments I was accustomed to using, and so I spent months developing a new approach that was based on free-hand drawings. I have been inspired by the work of Kevin Kallaugher, Ann Telnaes and Seth Tobocman (among the many artists I have had the good fortune to meet) and their commitment to free-hand drawings and the use of recurring characters. For their help and support, I thank Nancy Sadiq, Athar Hodali, Faris Sabaaneh, Thamer Sabaaneh, Dr. Waleed Deeb, Dr. Nahed Habiballah, Miko Peled, and the Arab American University.

1

HISTORY MATTERS

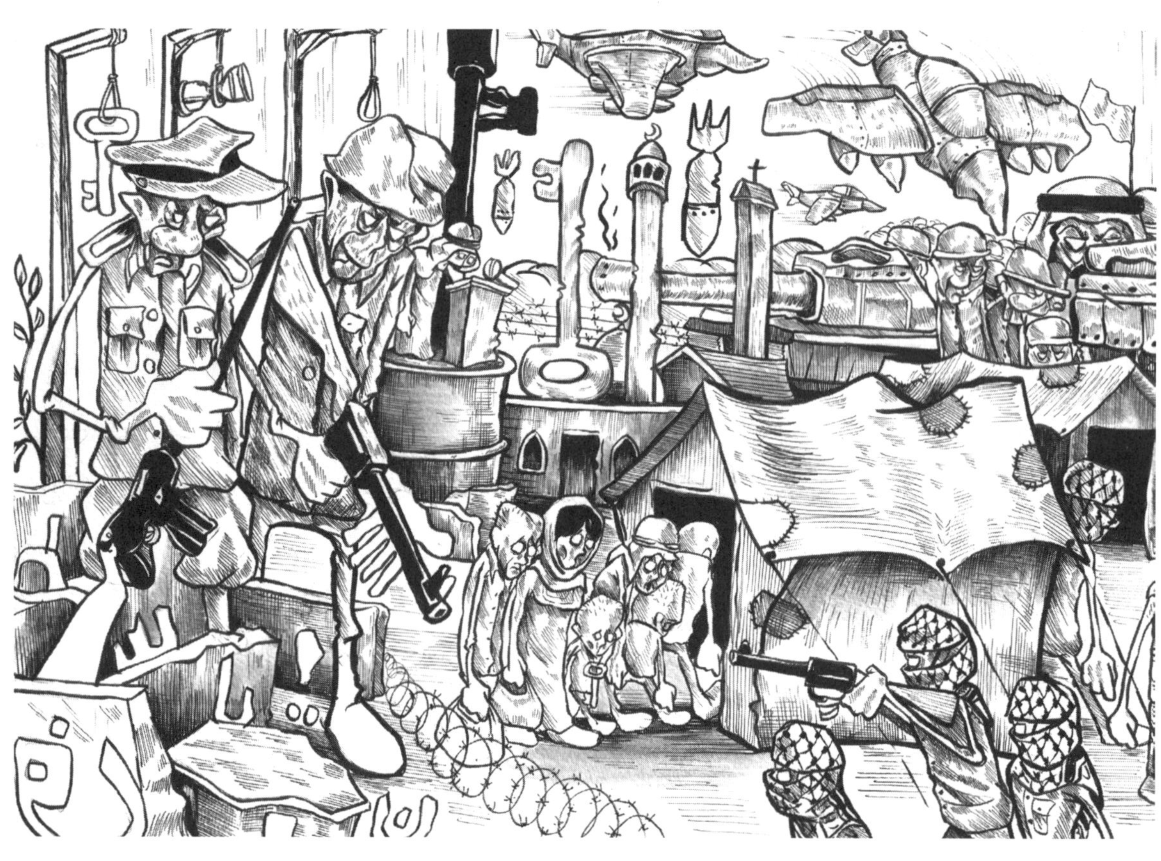

1922–65

The British Mandate, the Nakba, and Palestinian resistance

In 1922, the League of Nations gave Britain a 'Mandate' to govern Palestine. Under Britain's rule, Zionist colonisation accelerated. When Palestinians resisted, the British military countered with collective punishments, home demolitions, and public hangings. In 1947–48, as the British withdrew, Zionist militias expelled 750,000 Palestinians from the area in which they established a Jewish state, a process that Palestinians refer to as the Nakba, or catastrophe. After many years of hoping that diplomacy would win their UN promised 'Right of Return,' exiled Palestinians formed their own liberation movements to achieve this.

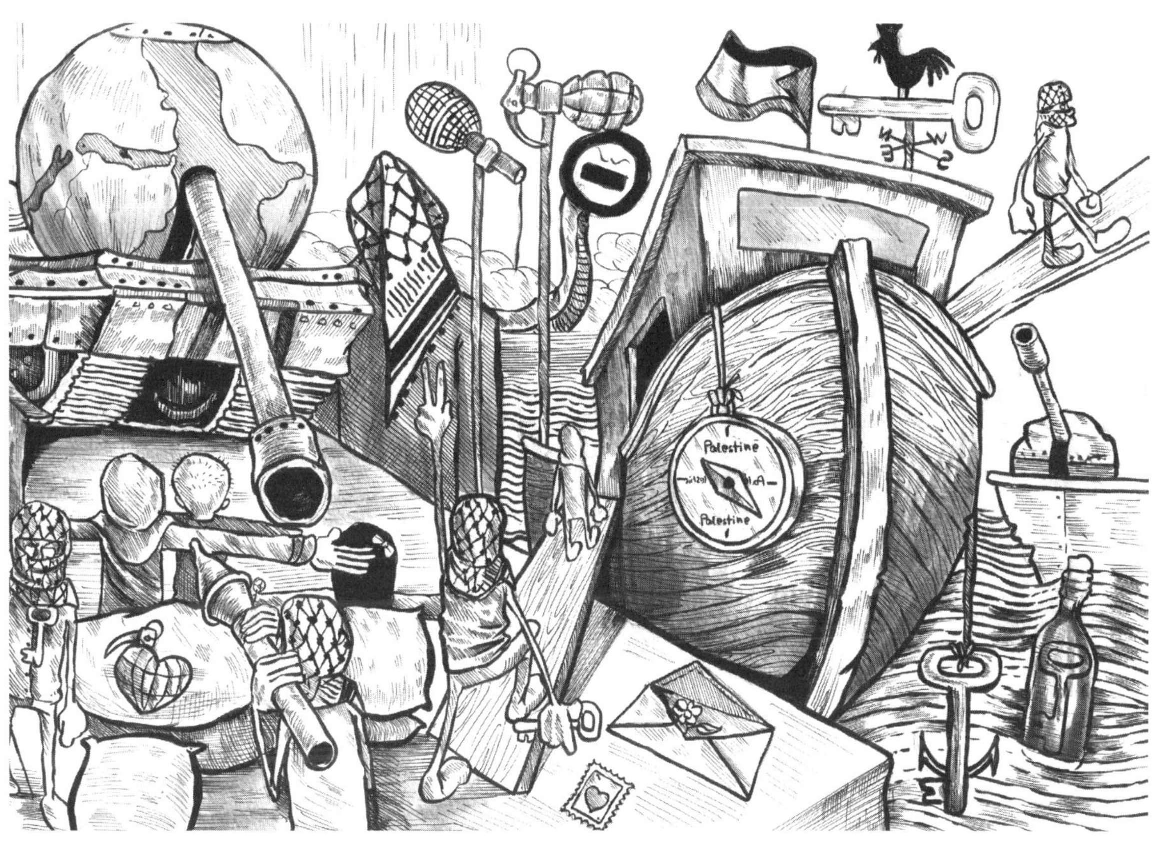

In June 1982, Israel invaded Lebanon to destroy the Palestinian Liberation Organization (PLO), which was then based there. After a two-month-long Israeli siege and bombardment of Beirut, the PLO accepted a US-brokered ceasefire. It stipulated that the Palestinian fighters should leave Beirut by sea, going to Arab countries far from Israel, and included Washington's guarantee that unarmed Palestinians left in the refugee camps near Beirut would be safe. Within weeks Israel orchestrated the entry of sharply anti-Palestinian militias into the Sabra and Shatila camps, where they slaughtered at least 1,500 residents.

1982

Israel's invasion of Lebanon and expulsion of the PLO

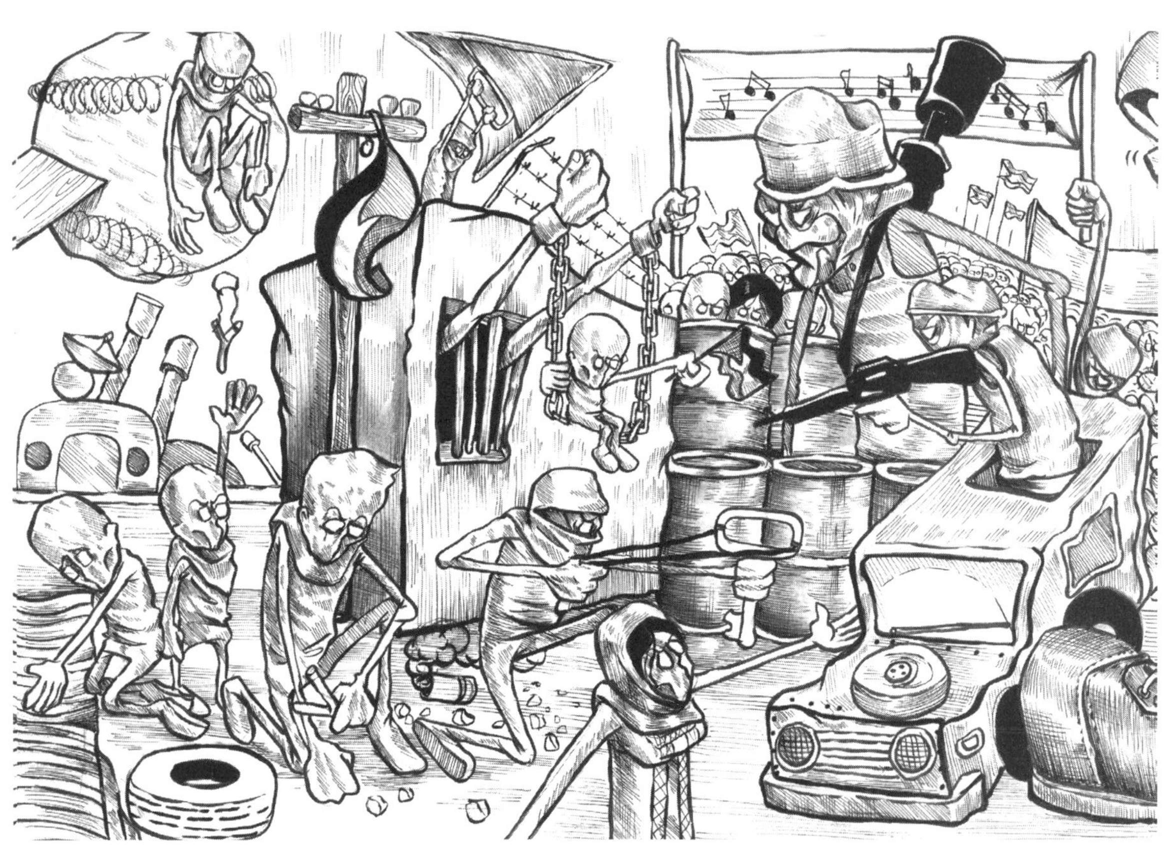

1987

The start of the first intifada

In late 1987, Palestinians in the West Bank and Gaza launched a nearly wholly nonviolent intifada, or uprising, against Israel's 20-year military occupation. They undertook many creative acts of civil disobedience, such as general strikes, mass demonstrations, and boycotts of Israeli products. In response, Israel shot demonstrators, imposed curfews, launched broad campaigns of imprisonment, closed schools and universities, deported suspected ringleaders, and used intentional tactics of 'breaking their bones.' By the end of the intifada's first year, 405 Palestinians had been killed, 20,000 injured, 20,000 arrested, and 32 deported.

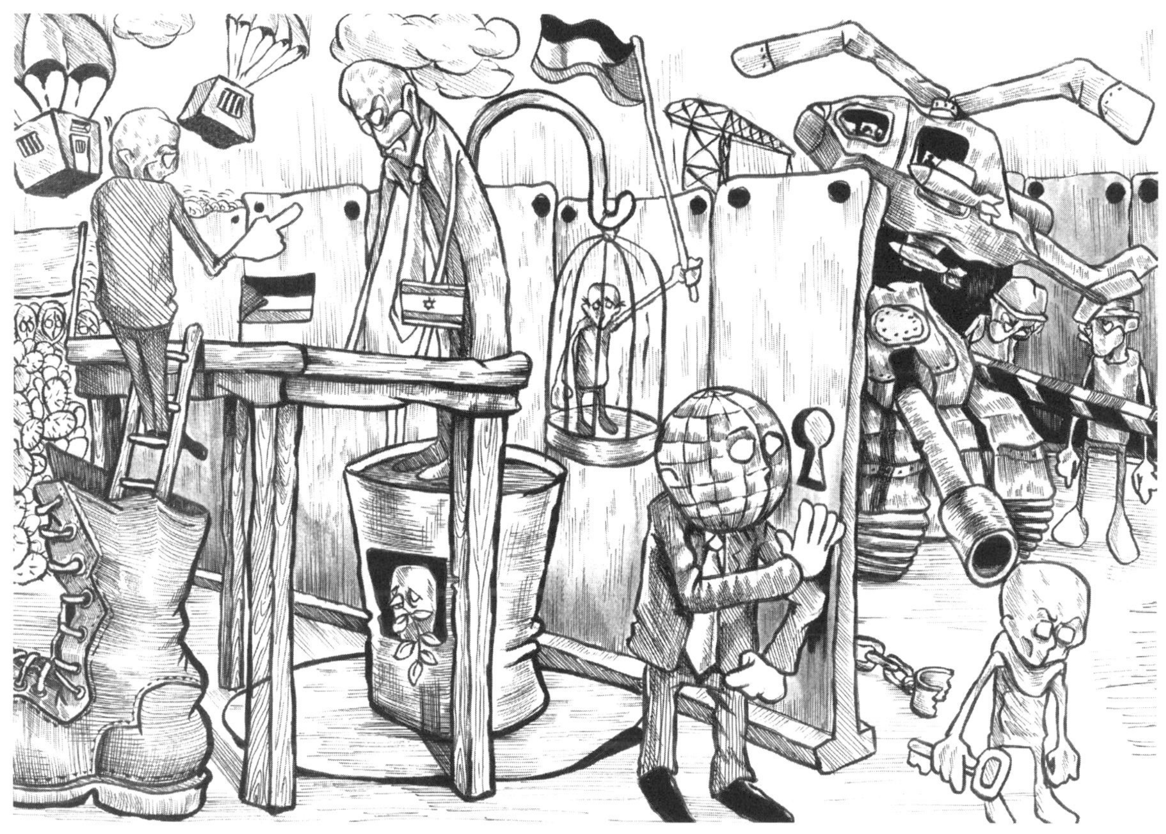

In 1993, the PLO and Israel signed the Oslo Accord. It allowed some PLO leaders to enter the West Bank and Gaza to create an interim Palestinian Authority, but under firm Israeli control. A final peace was supposed to be negotiated by 1999. But Israel intensified its illegal construction of settlements, and the peace talks led nowhere. In September 2000, Palestinians launched a second intifada. Israel responded with familiar violence. Claiming security needs, Israel started building a massive wall that cut many West Bank Palestinian communities off from each other. The wall, along with Israeli settlements, curfews, and checkpoints, radically constrains Palestinians' daily life and economic activity.

1993–2004

The Palestinian Authority, a new intifada, Israel's Apartheid Wall

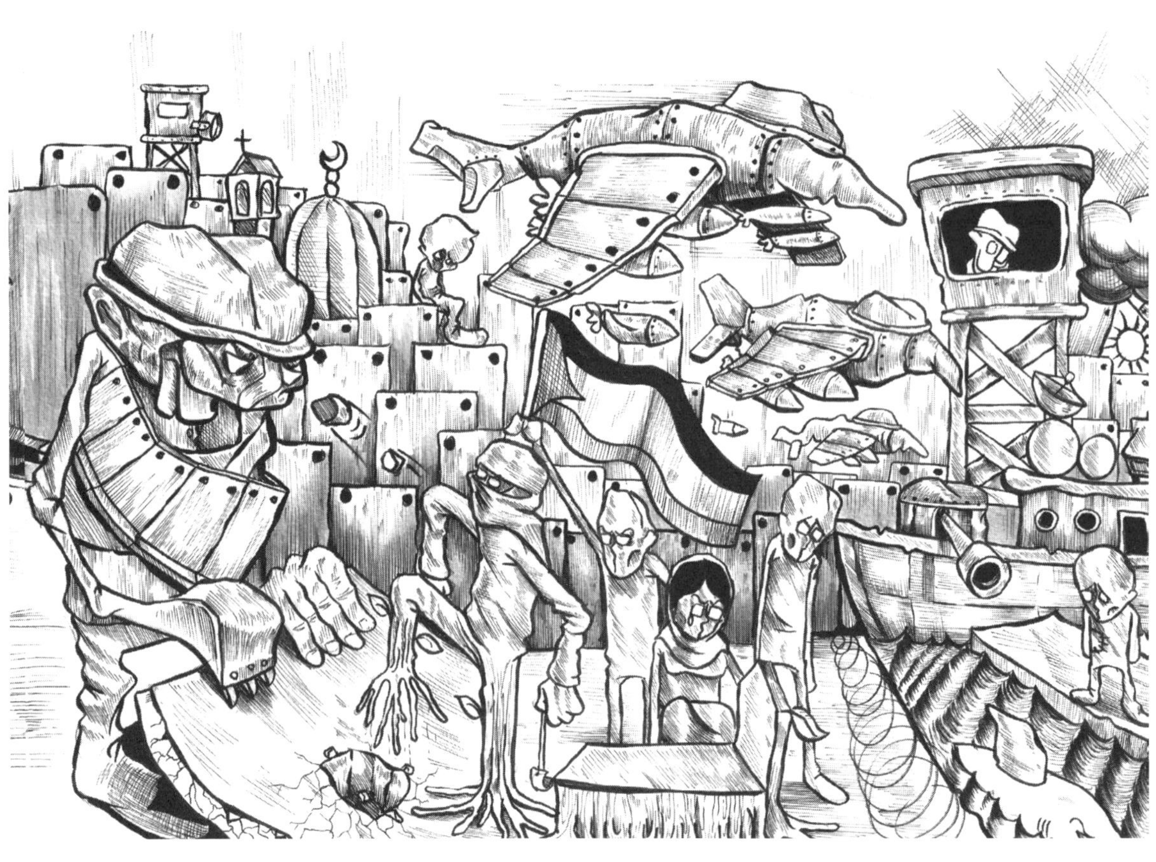

2004–14

Increased Israeli control of the West Bank, assaults on Gaza

Palestinians judge that the Oslo process is dead. They feel trapped in an endless, US-led process that lets Israel do as it pleases. Israel's land confiscation, settlement construction, and wall-building in the West Bank dice the terrain into ever smaller pieces. In 2005, Israel withdrew its settlers and soldiers from inside the Gaza Strip. That allowed it to launch broad, devastating military attacks against the Strip's two million Palestinians, which it did in 2008, 2012, and 2014. Those attacks, along with Israel's tight land and sea blockade of Gaza, have destroyed its economy, pushing many Gaza Palestinians into despair.

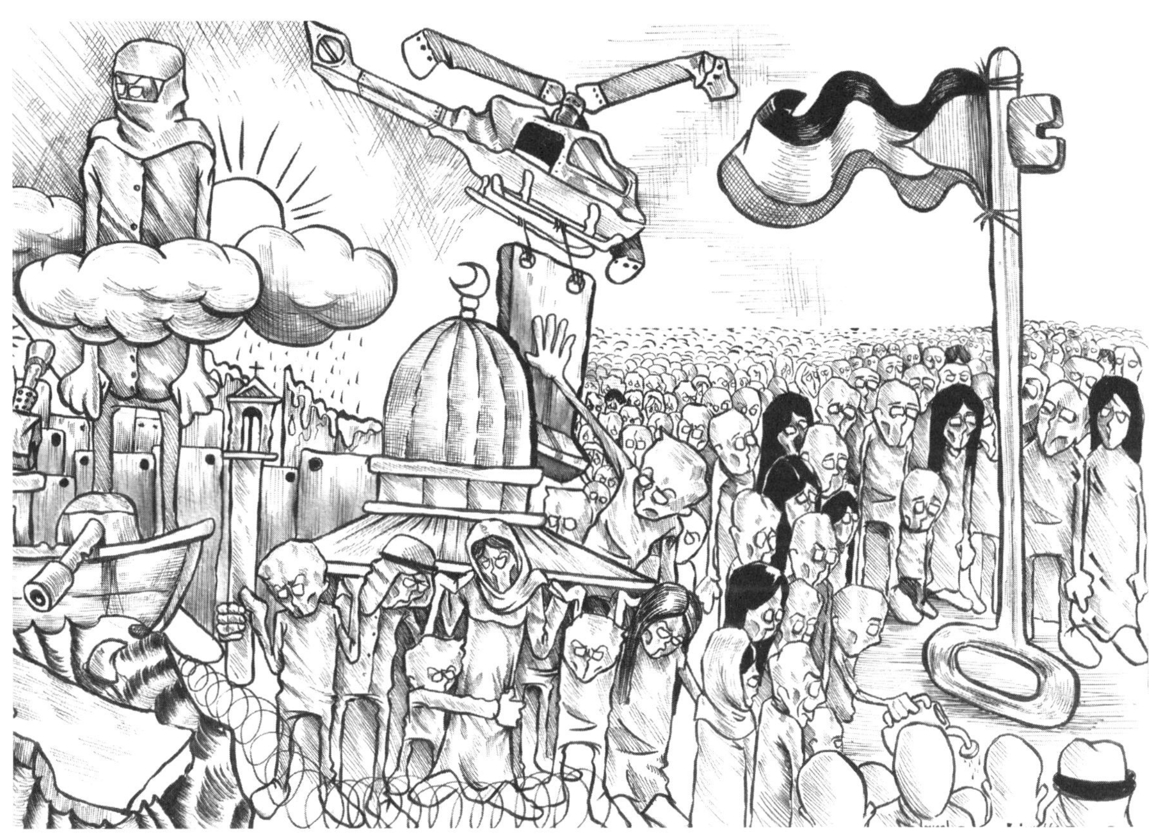

Israel accelerates its attacks against Jerusalem's Palestinians, increasing its demolition of their homes and revocation of their residency rights as it builds massive, Jewish-only settlements in East Jerusalem. The walling-off of East Jerusalem from its natural hinterland elsewhere in the West Bank continues. The Aqsa Mosque sees ongoing confrontations between Palestinians and Israeli soldiers who seek to restrict their access to it, and increasingly aggressive Zionist extremists aiming to replace it with a Jewish Temple. Meanwhile, Palestinians around the world reject as anachronistic the concept of a Jewish exclusivist state and continue to demand their Right of Return.

2015–16

Renewed attention to Jerusalem and the Right of Return

2

LIFE IN OCCUPIED PALESTINE

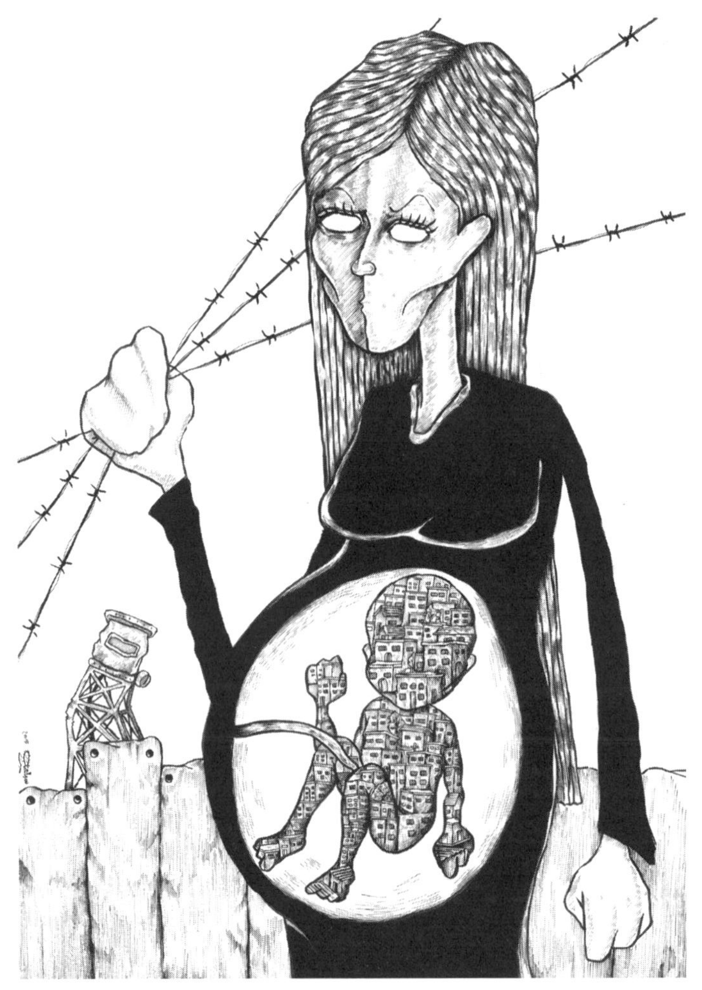

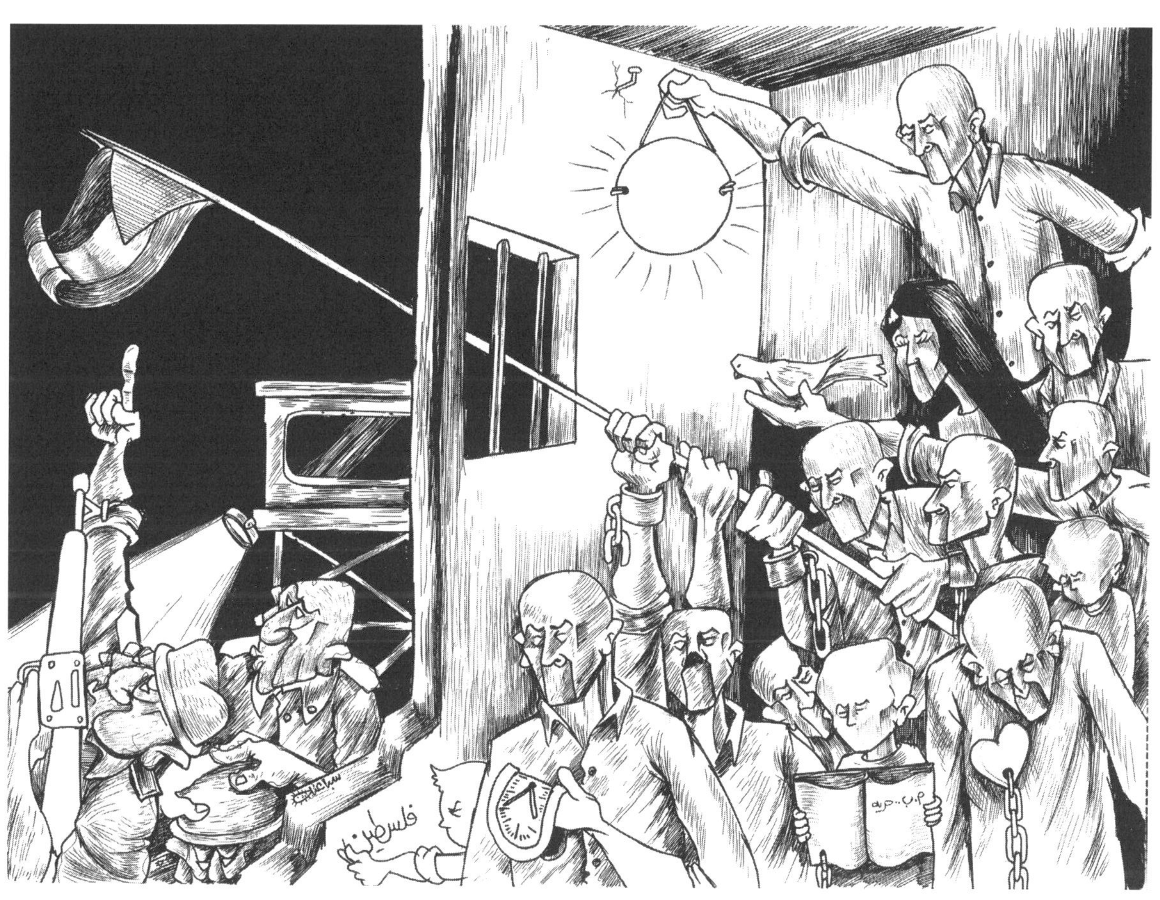

Political prisoners struggle for justice.

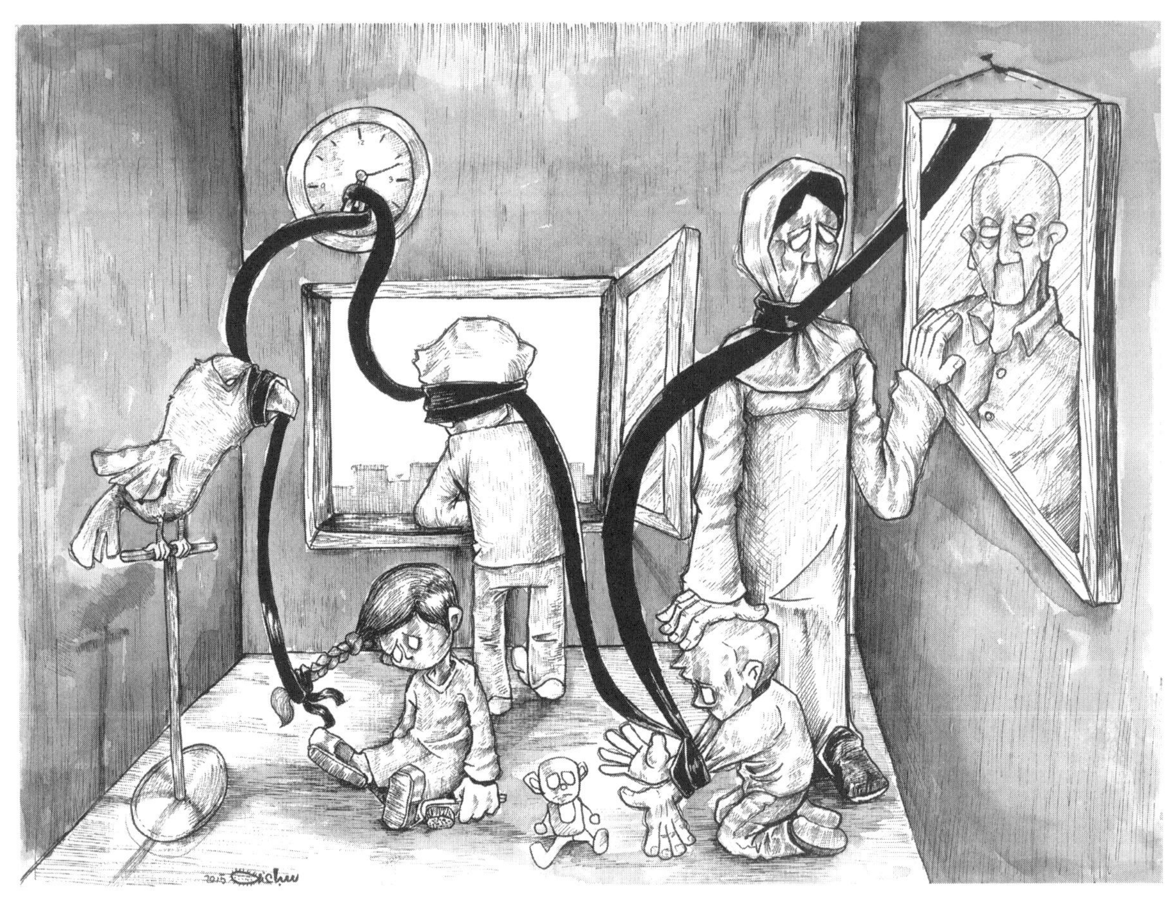

Connecting our stories, dreams, and sorrows.

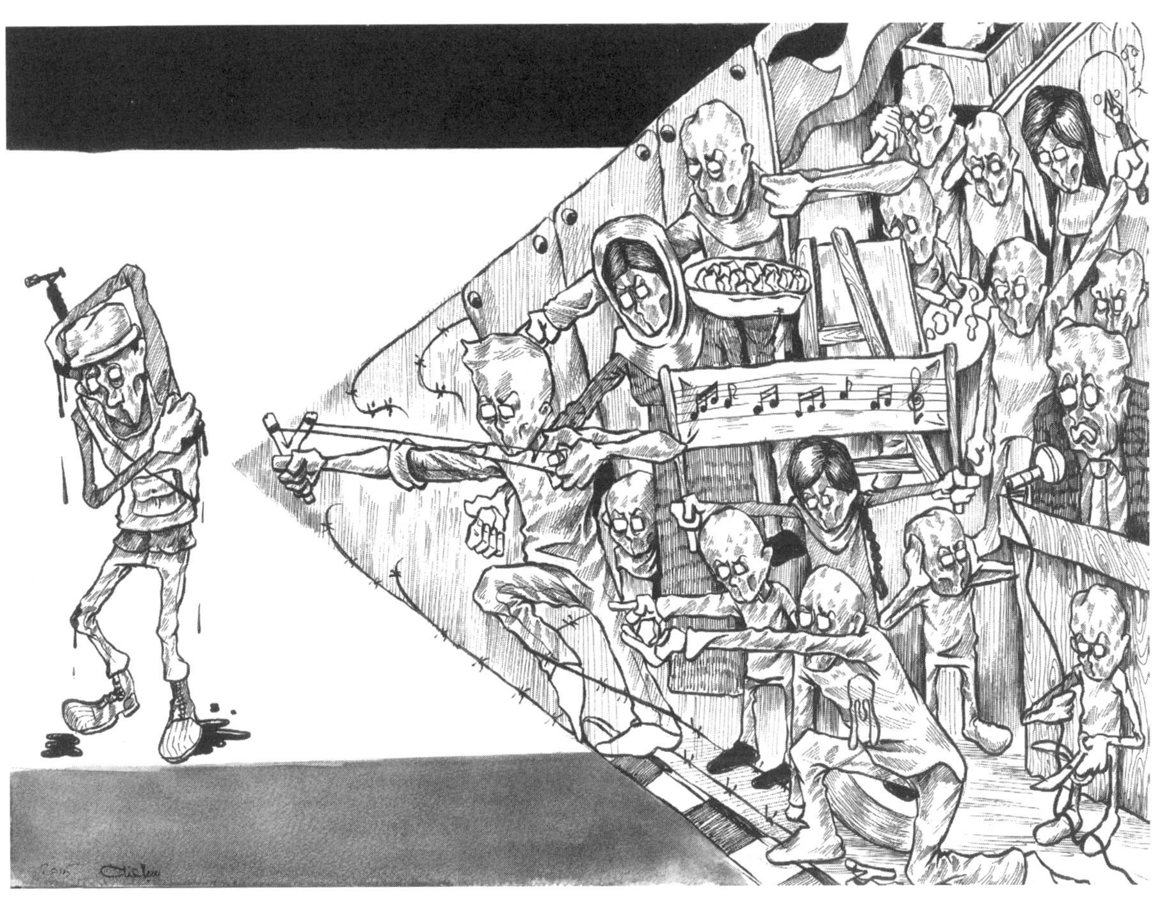

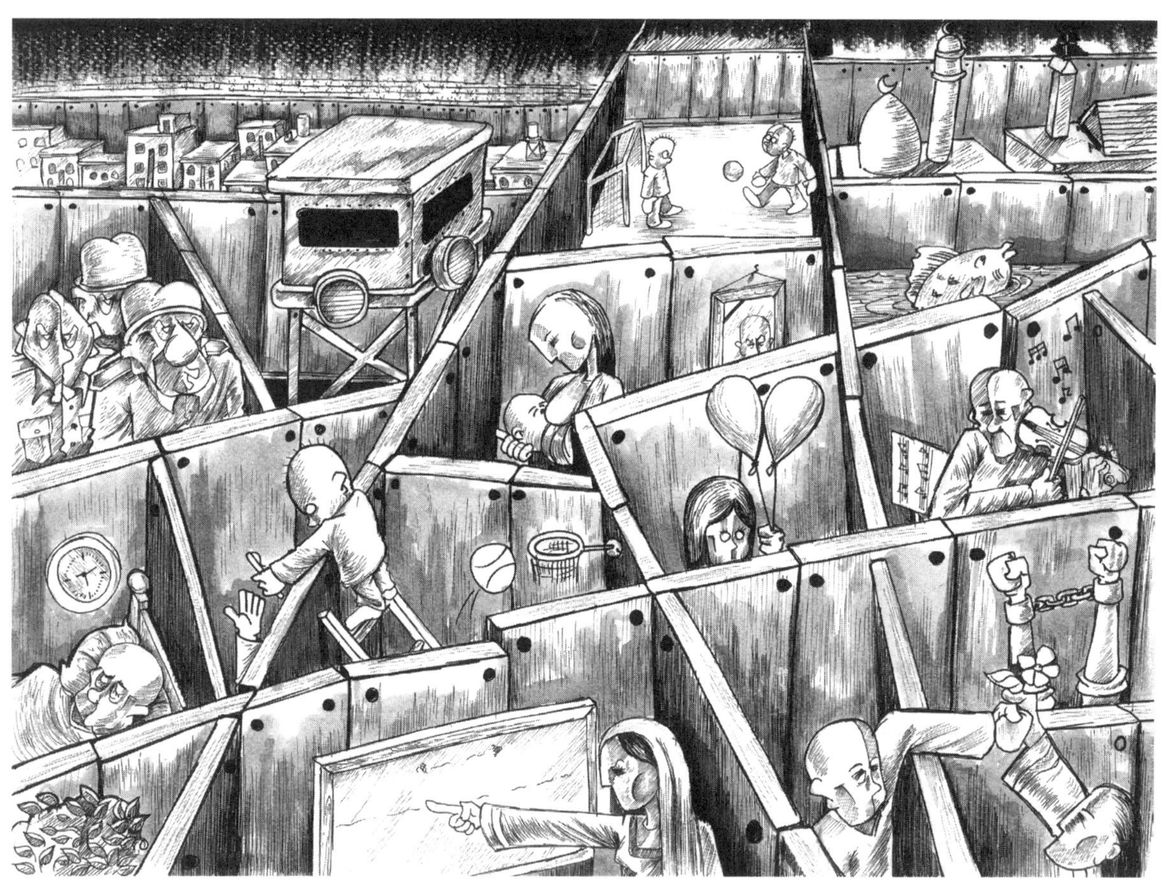

Lives interrupted.

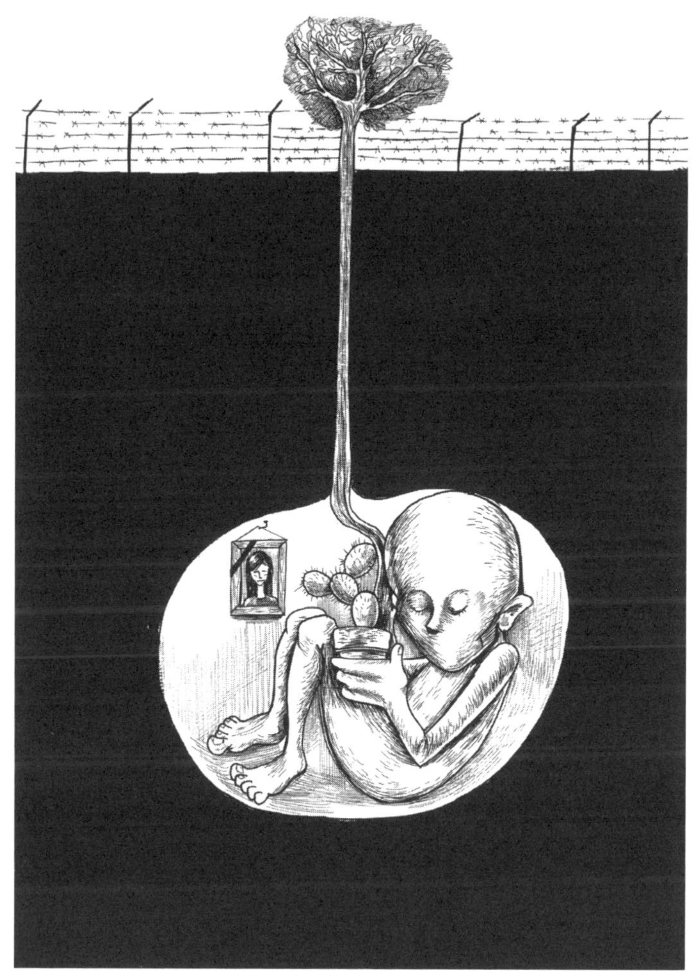

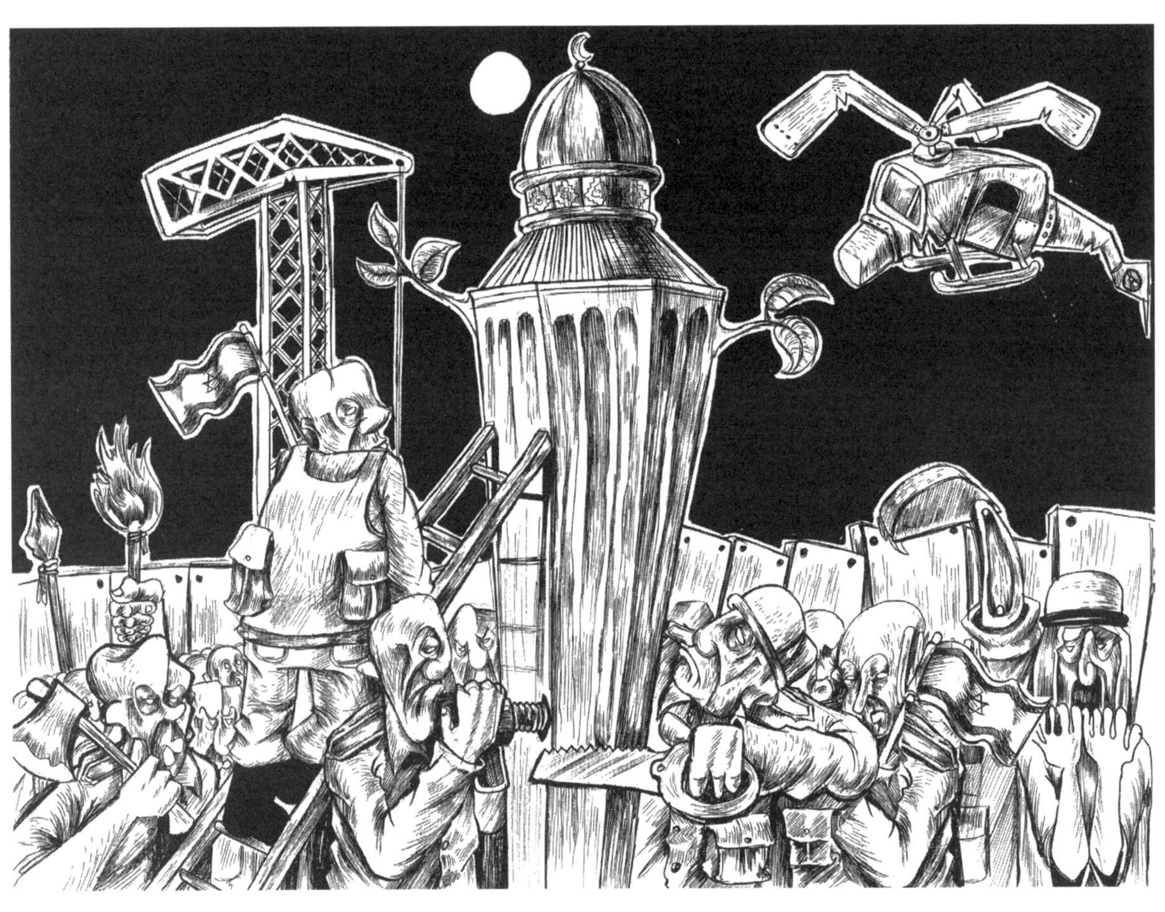

Jerusalem, the Holy Land.

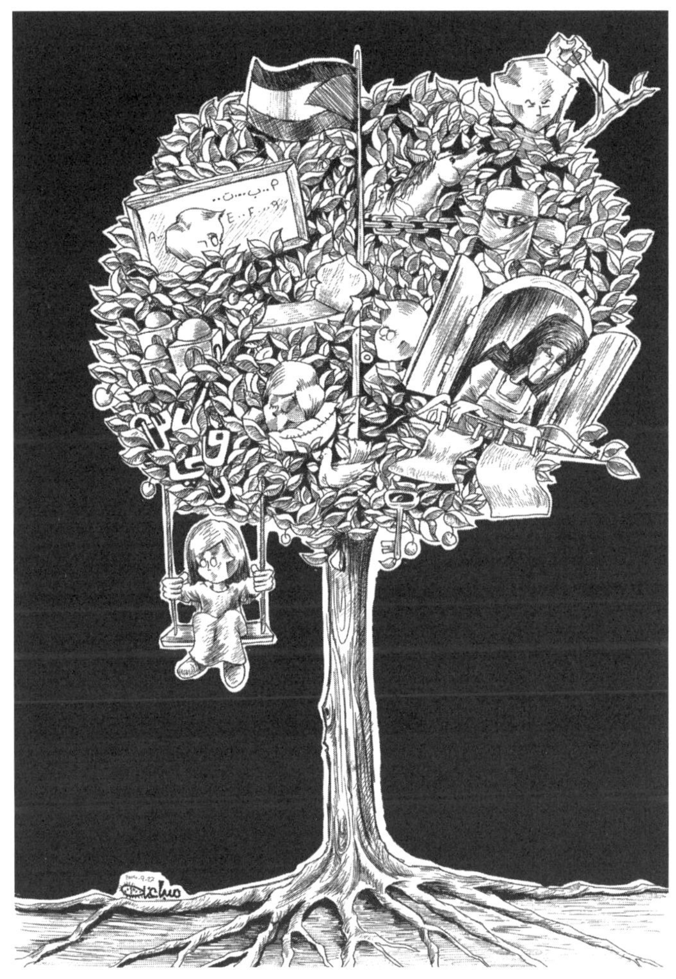

Protect your trees as though your lives depend on them.

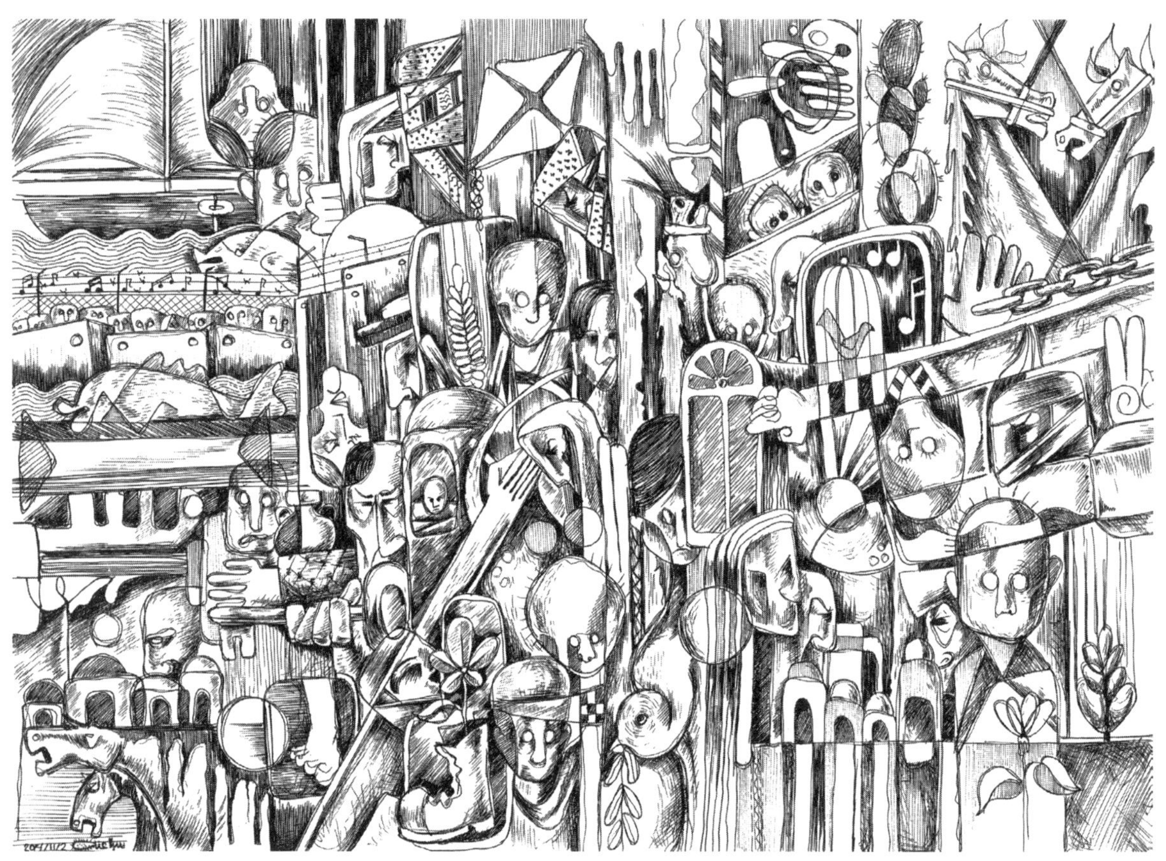

In the end, it's the 'us' that matters.

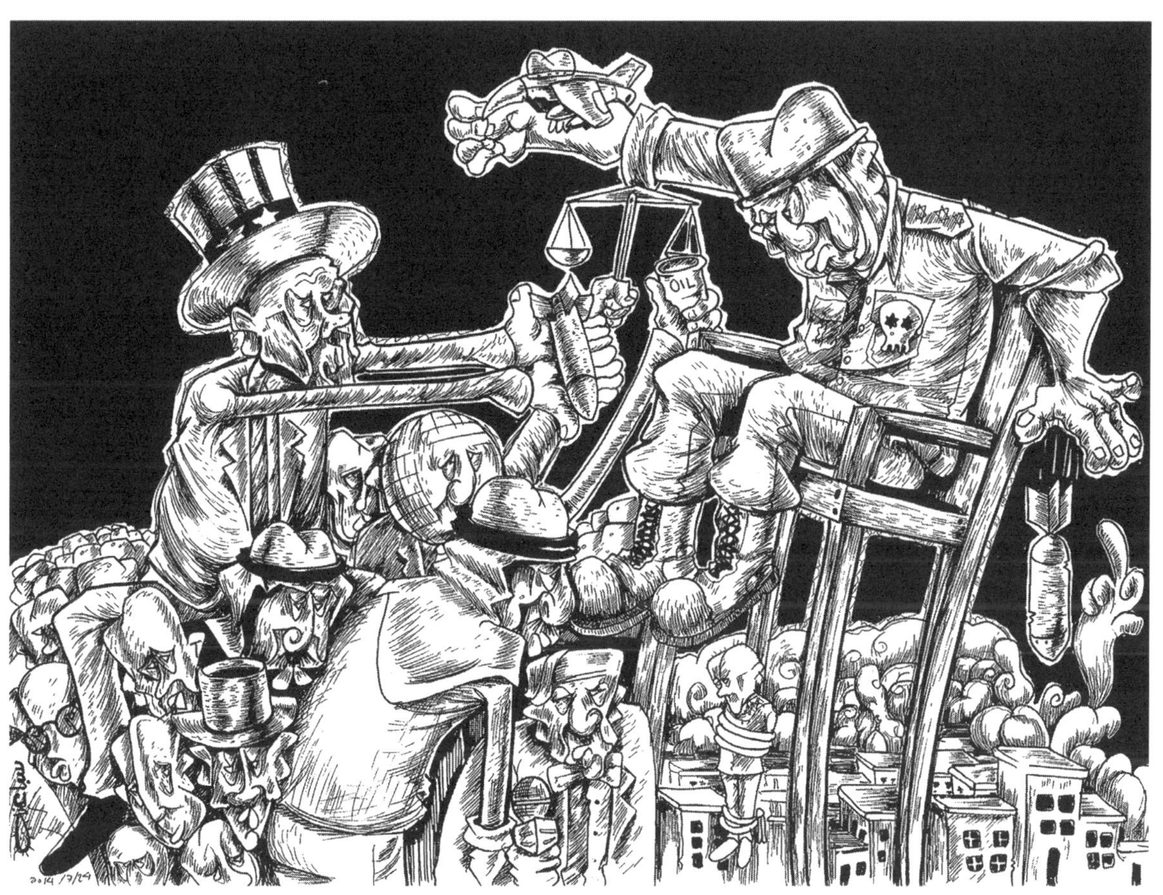

Tyrants are created and collectively sustained.

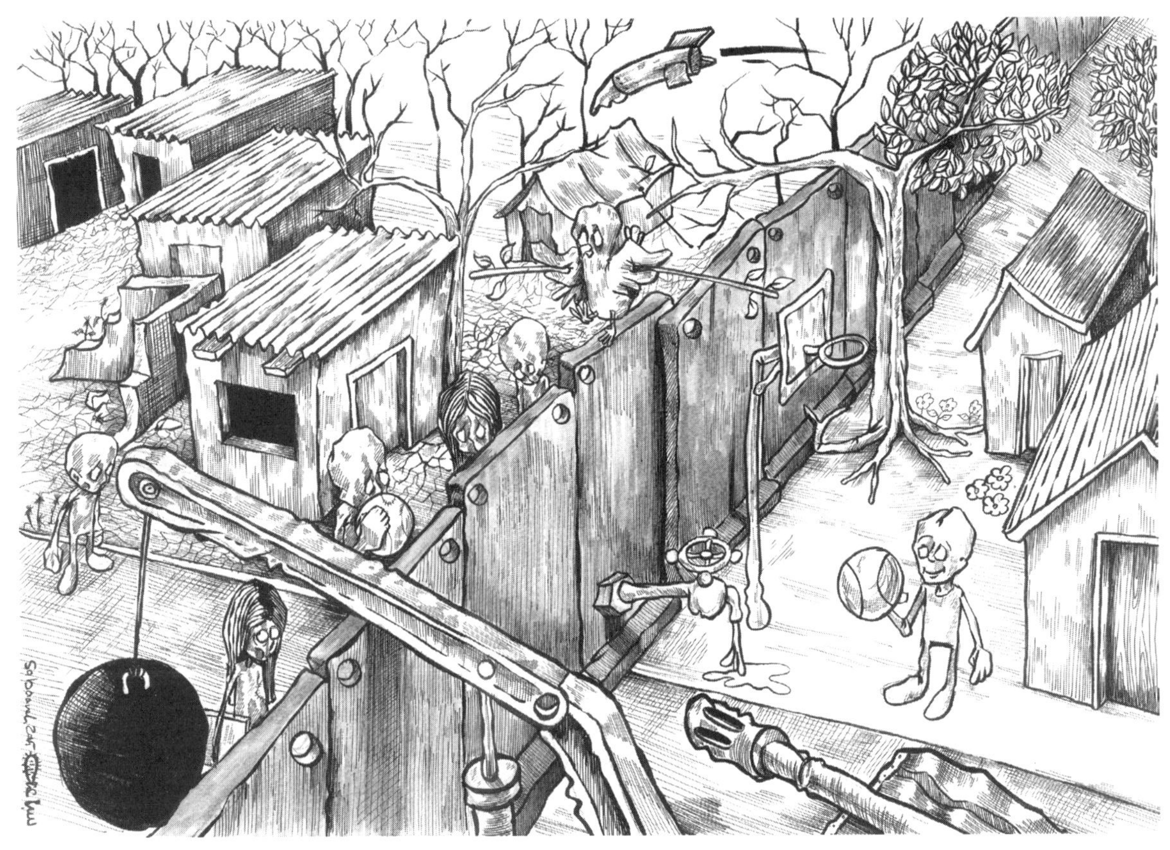

Keeping out the have-nots.

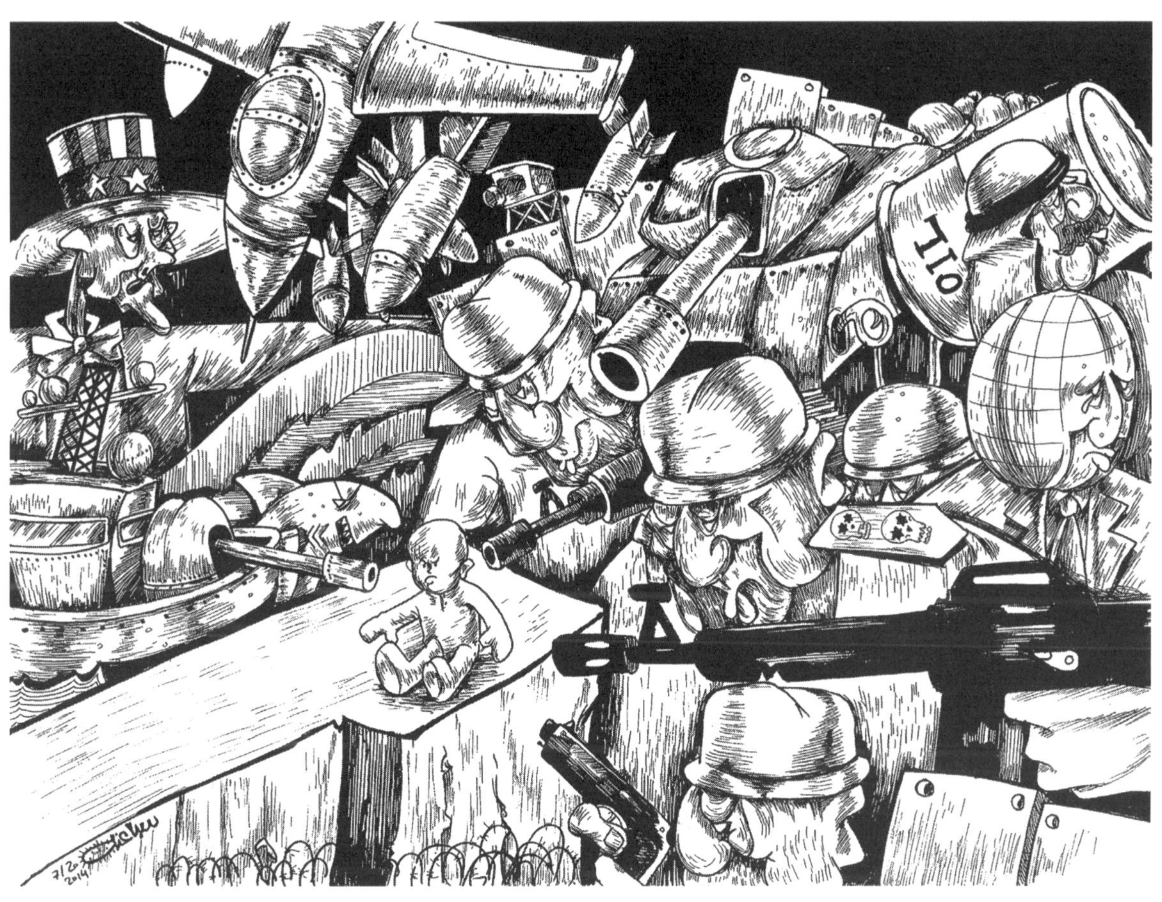
OIL

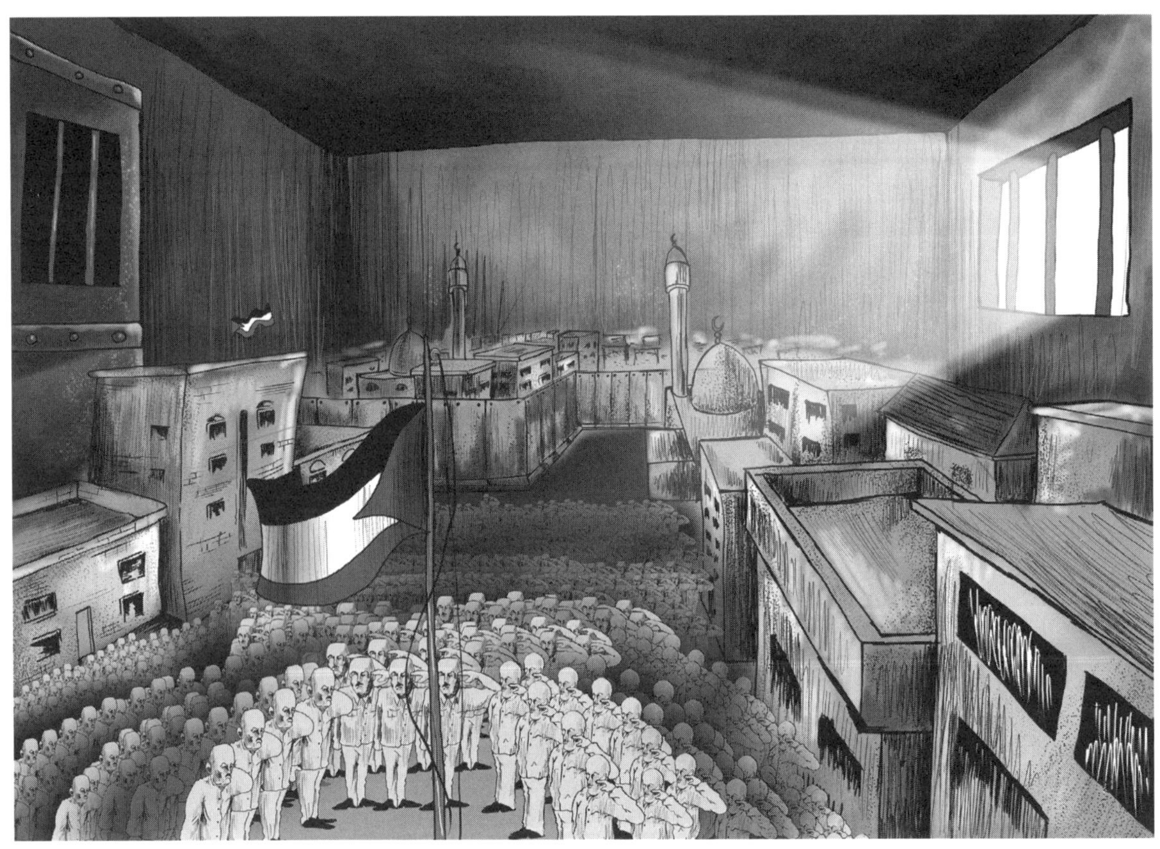

Foreign occupation and national institutions of statehood coexist in confined spaces.

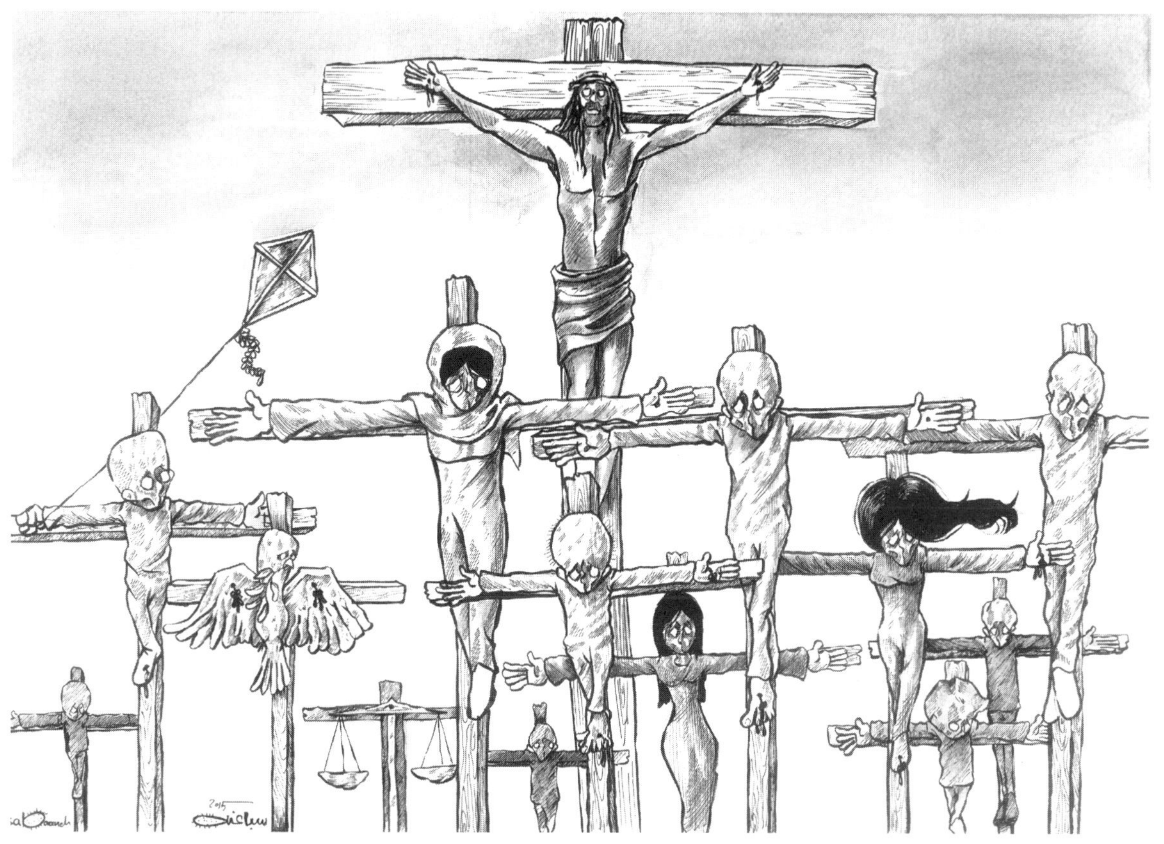

Golgotha today.

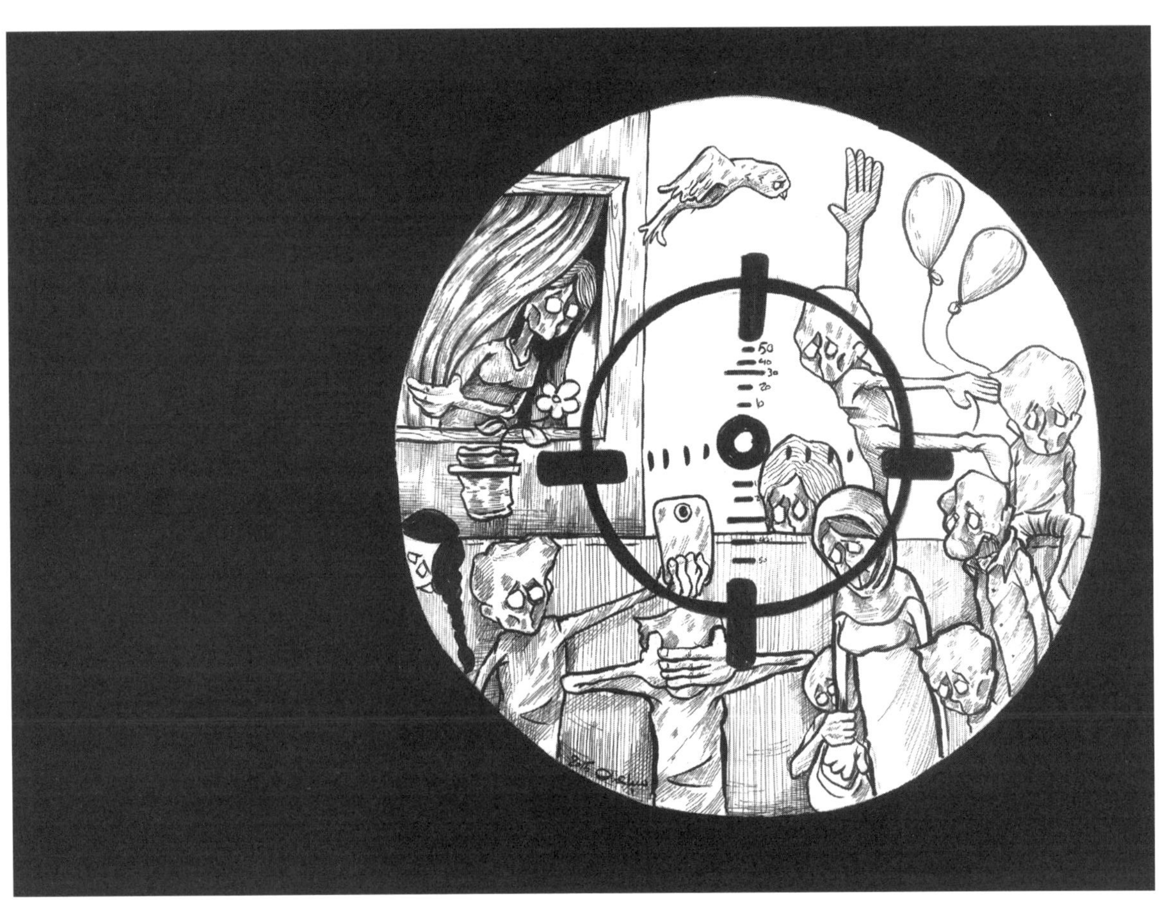

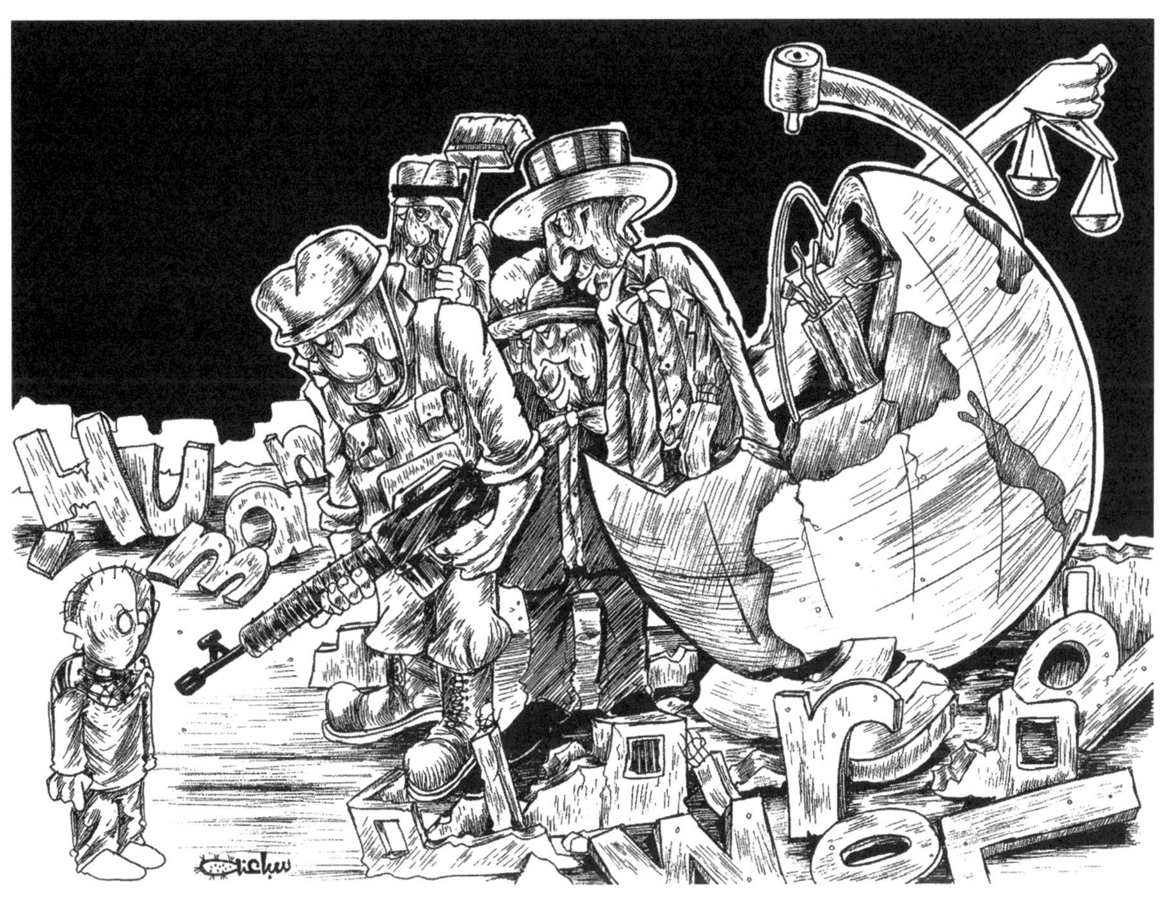

Identifying the real threat.

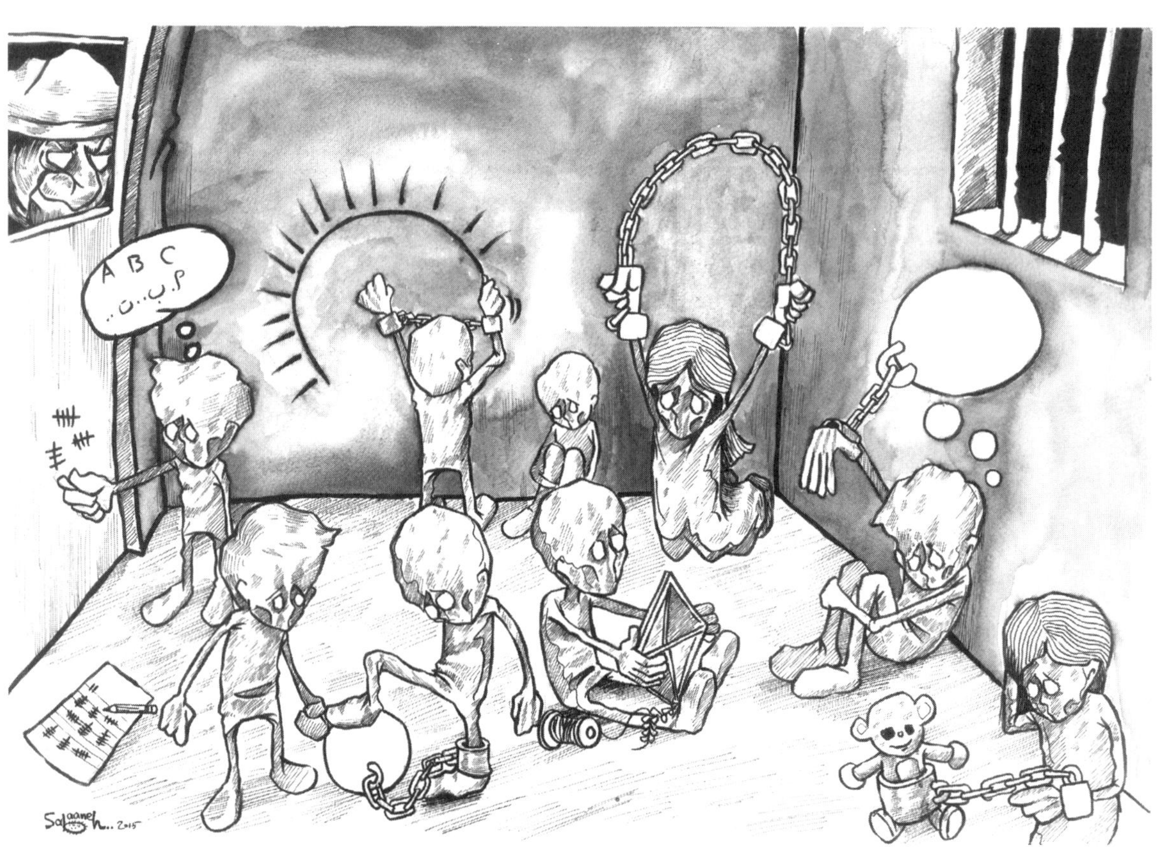

A B C
ا ب ت ث

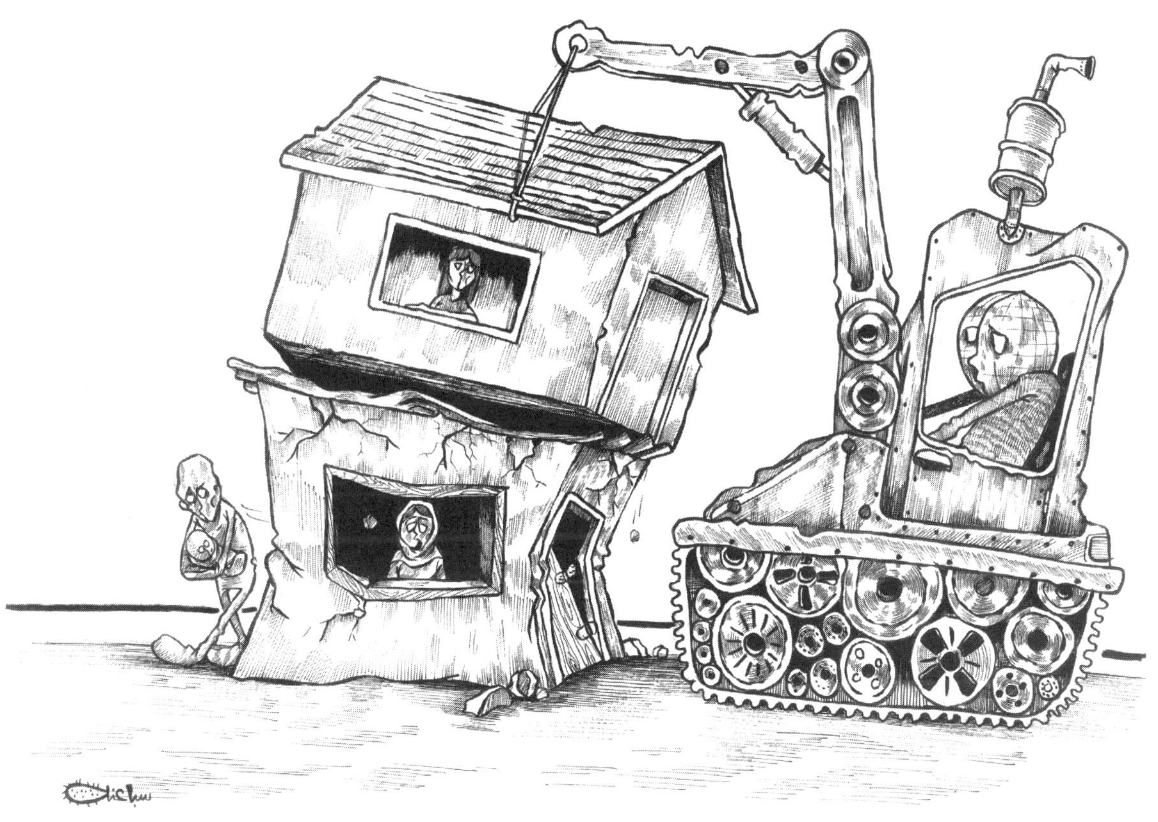

Replacing the indigenous population.

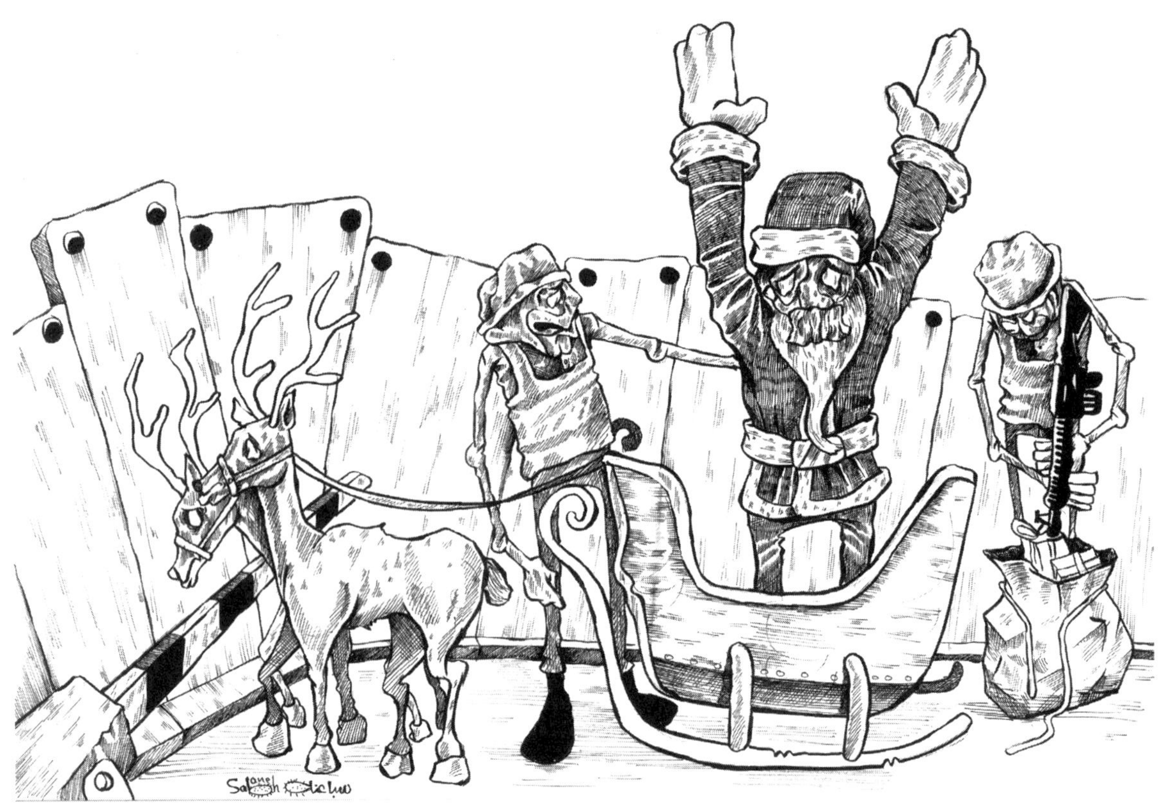

No exceptions.

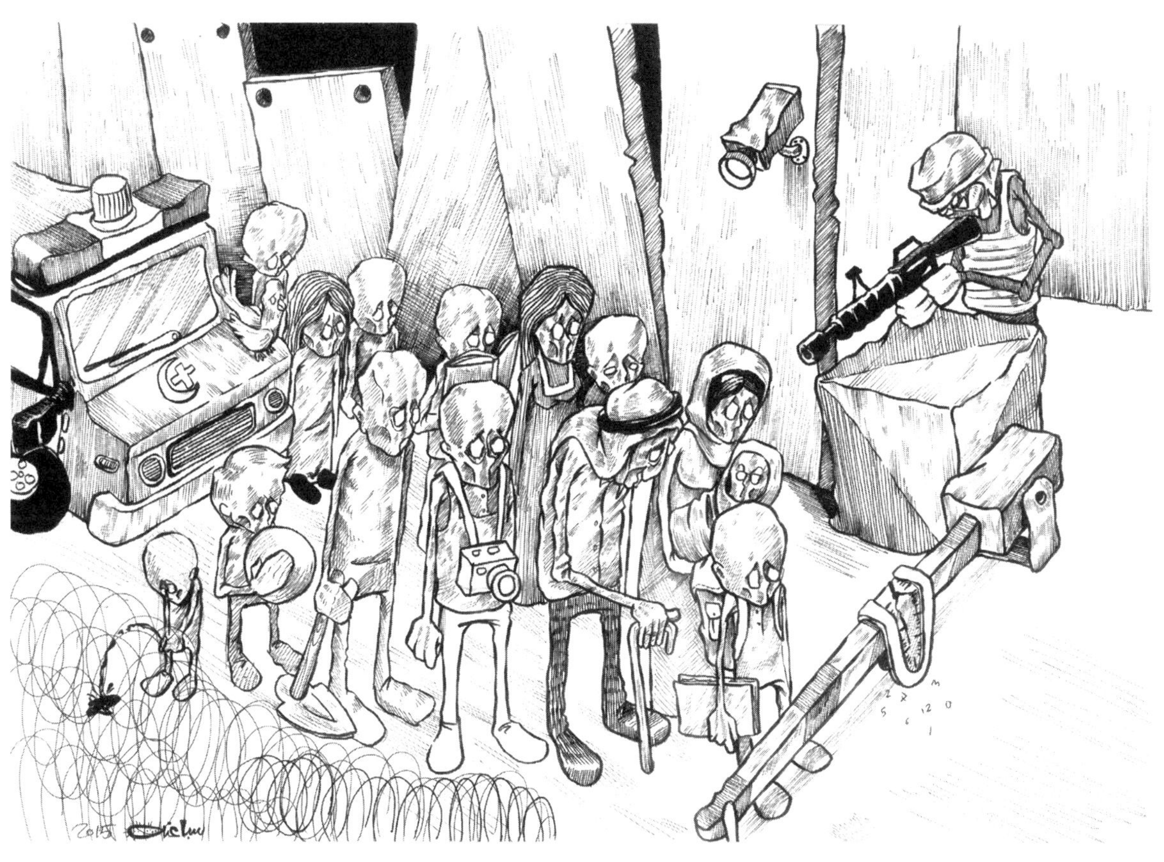

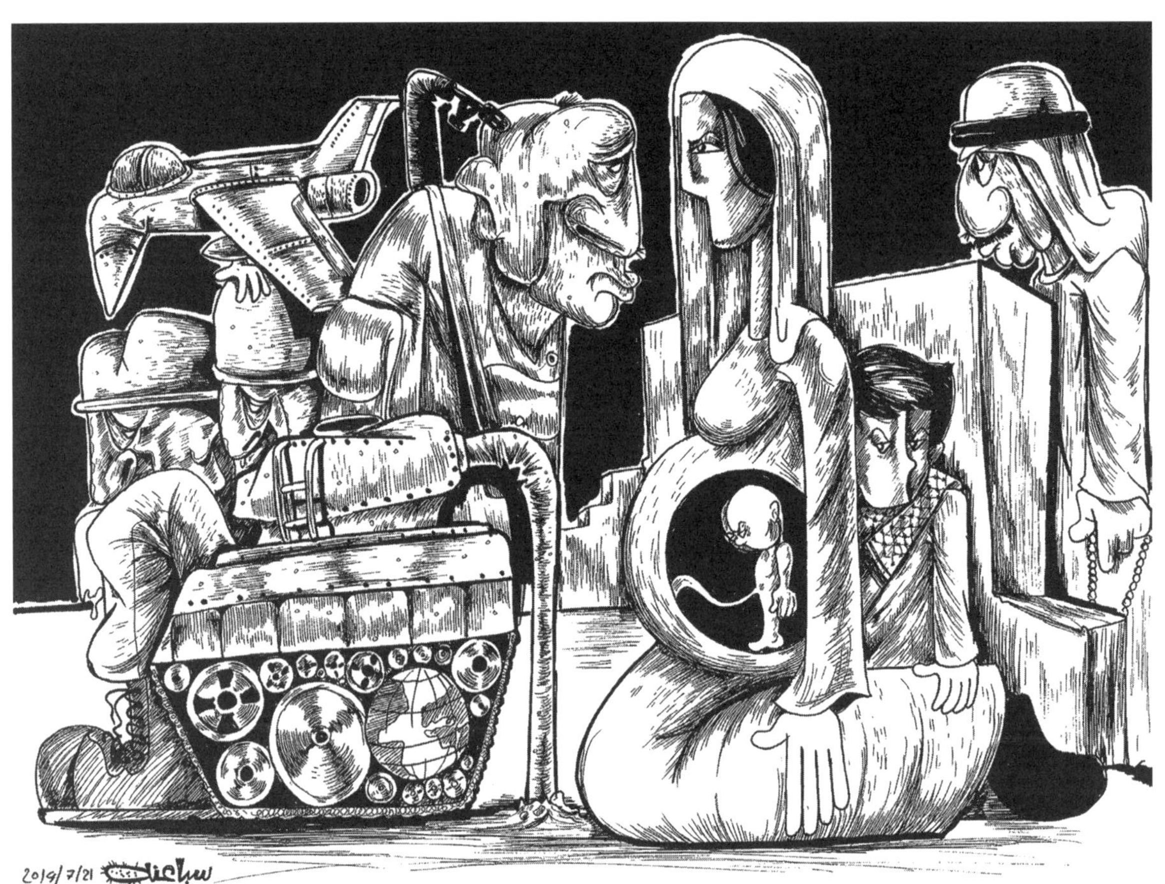

2019/ 7/21

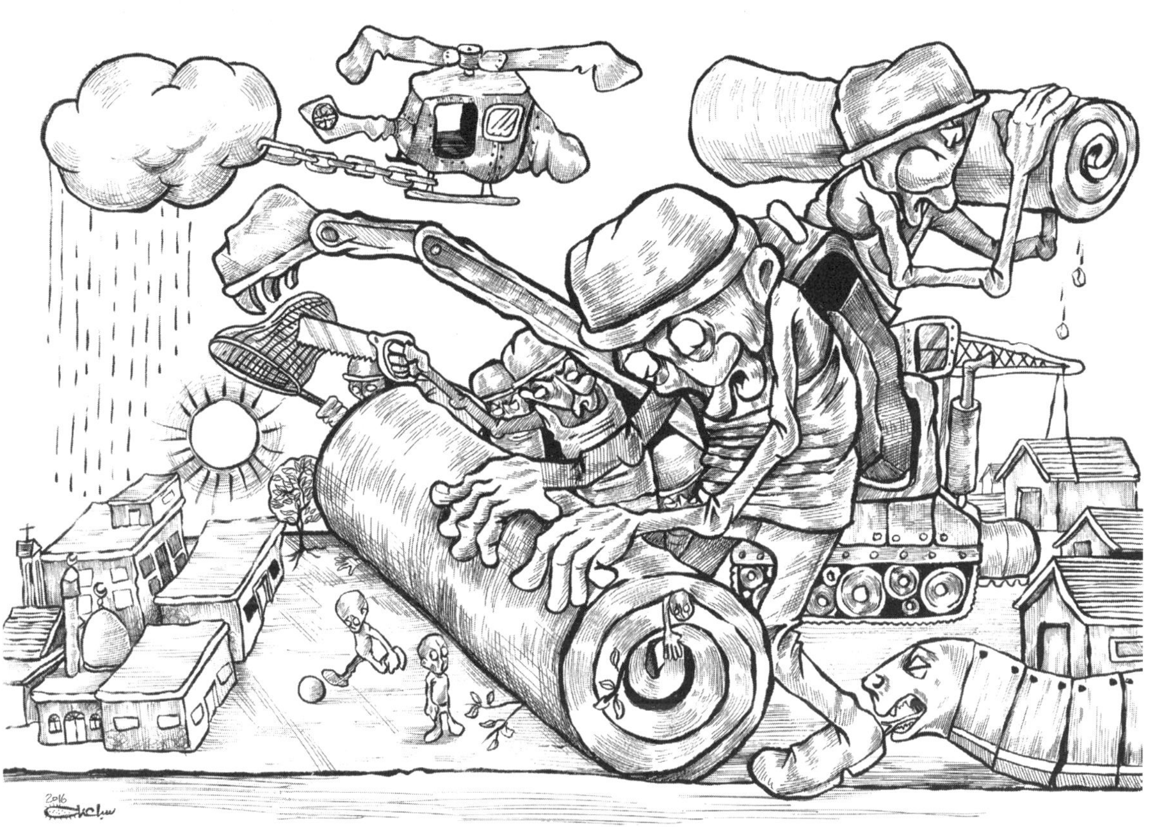

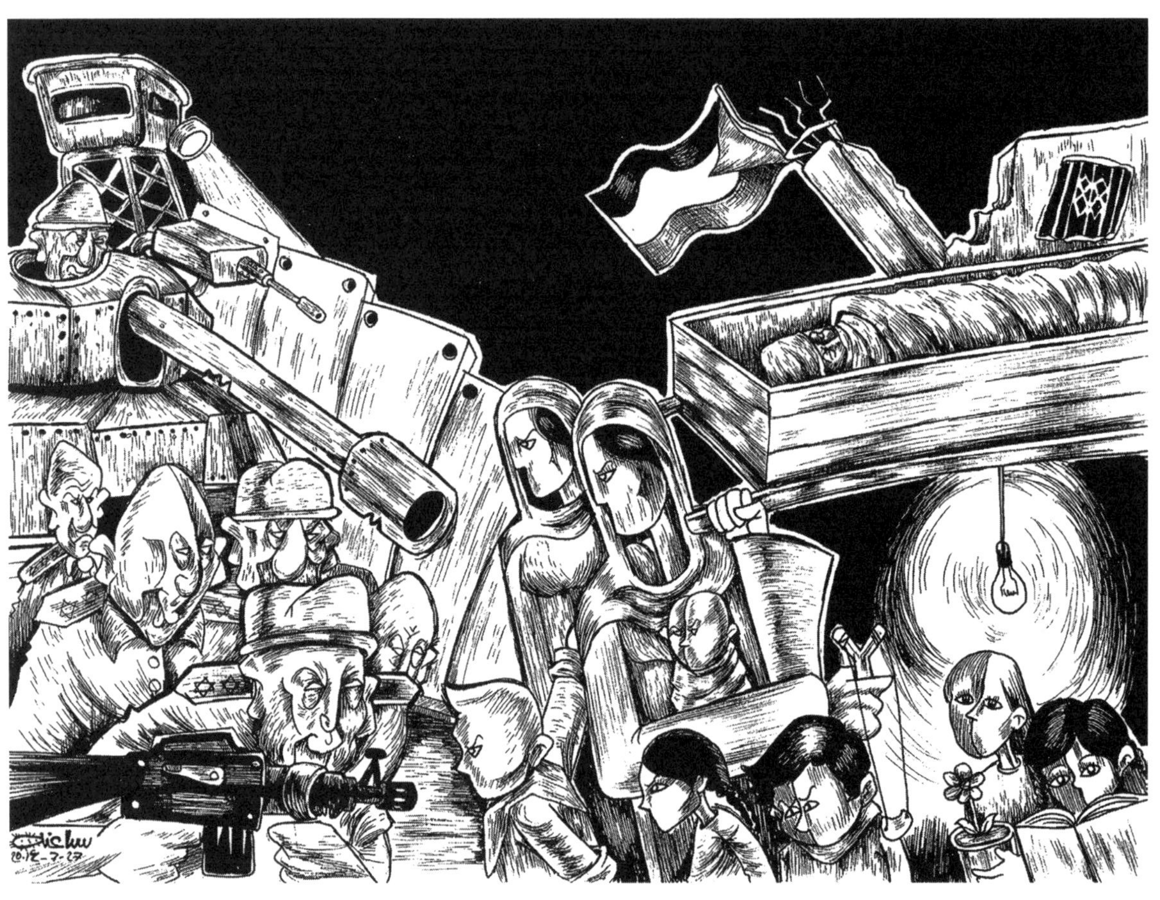

No peace for the dead either.

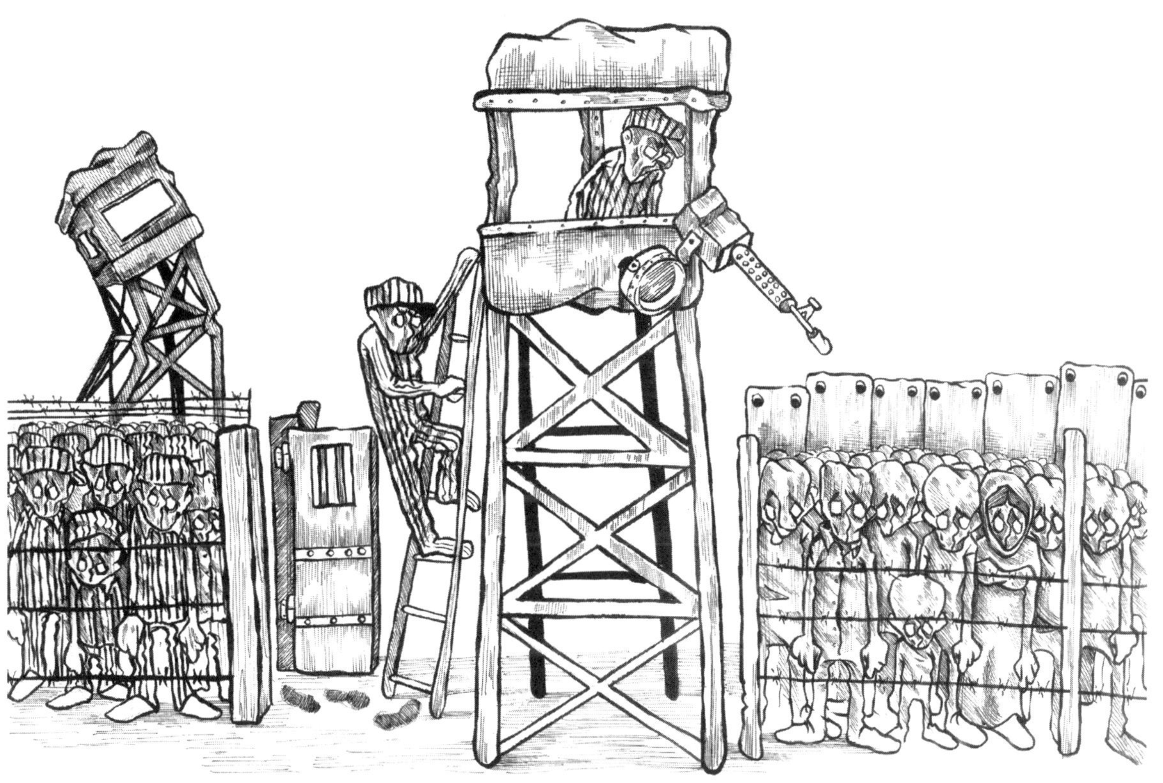

Metamorphosis.

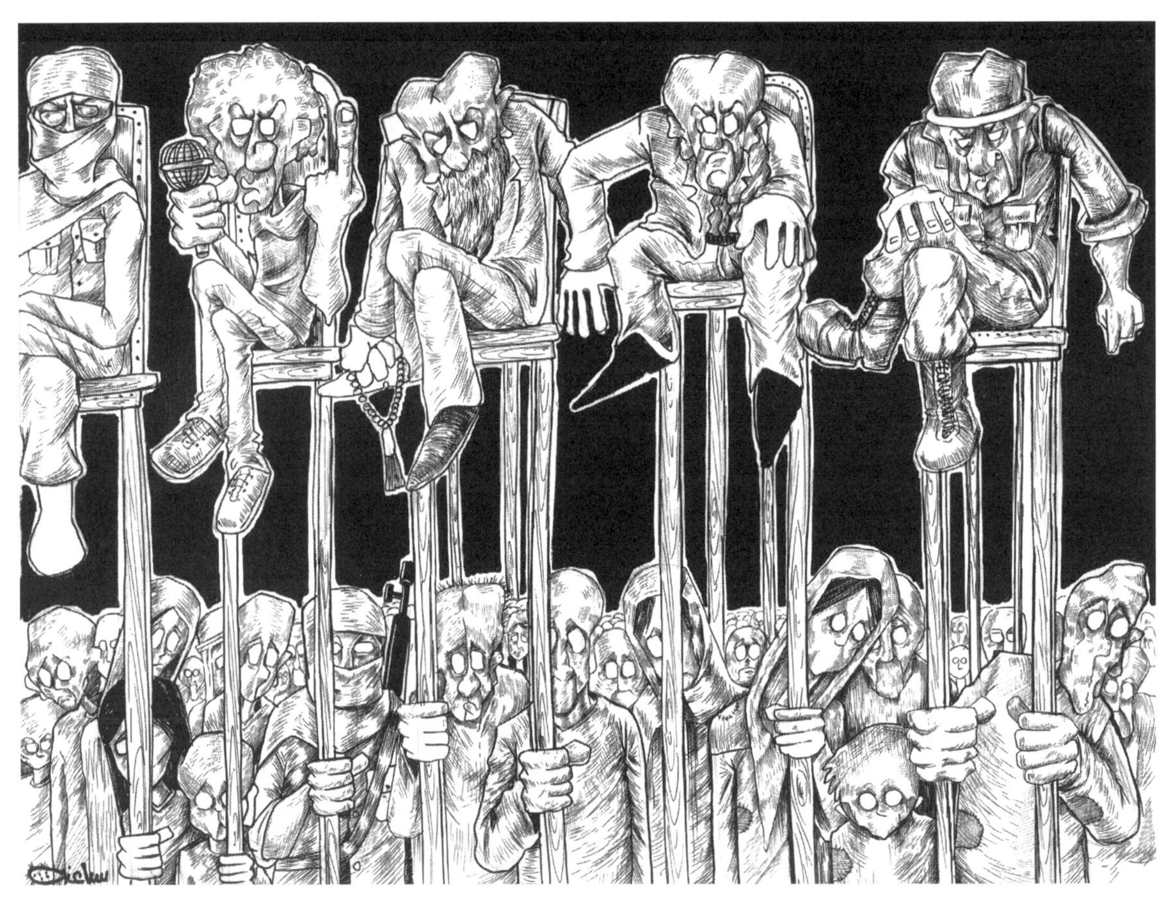

We create all types of oppressors.

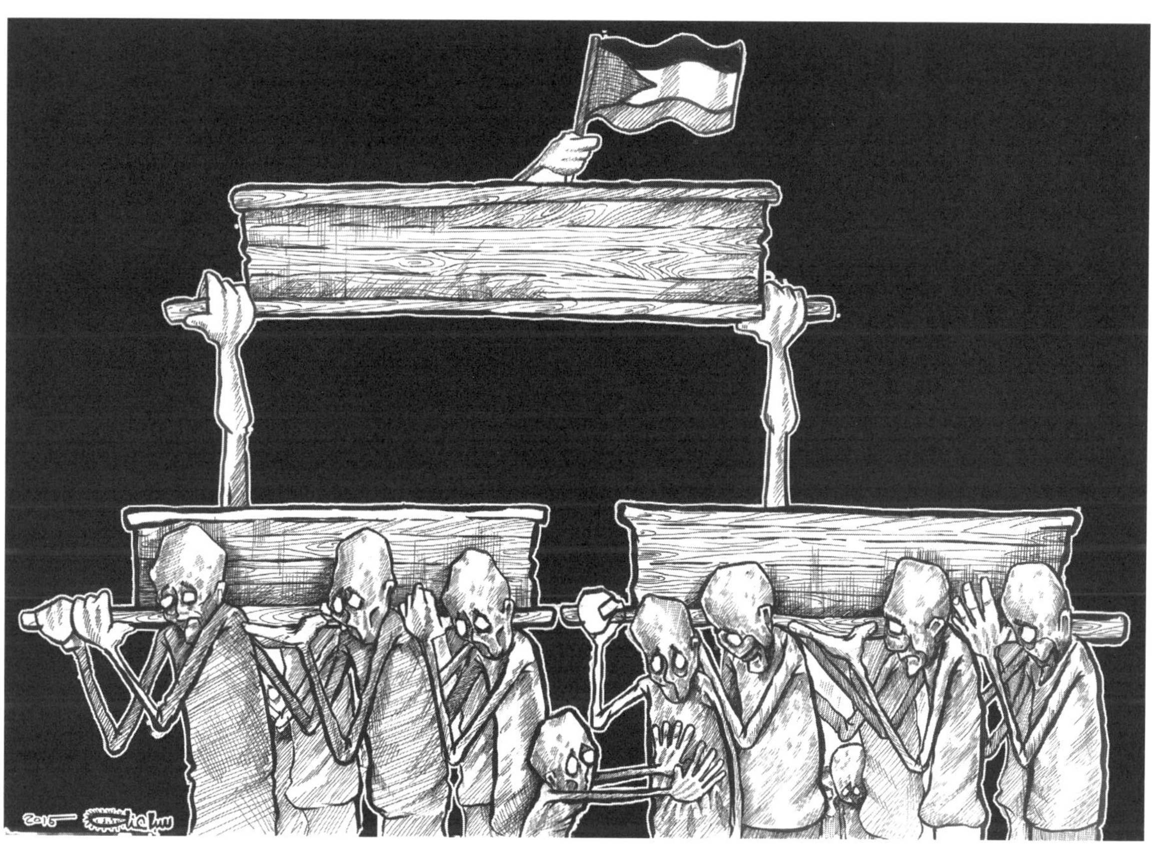

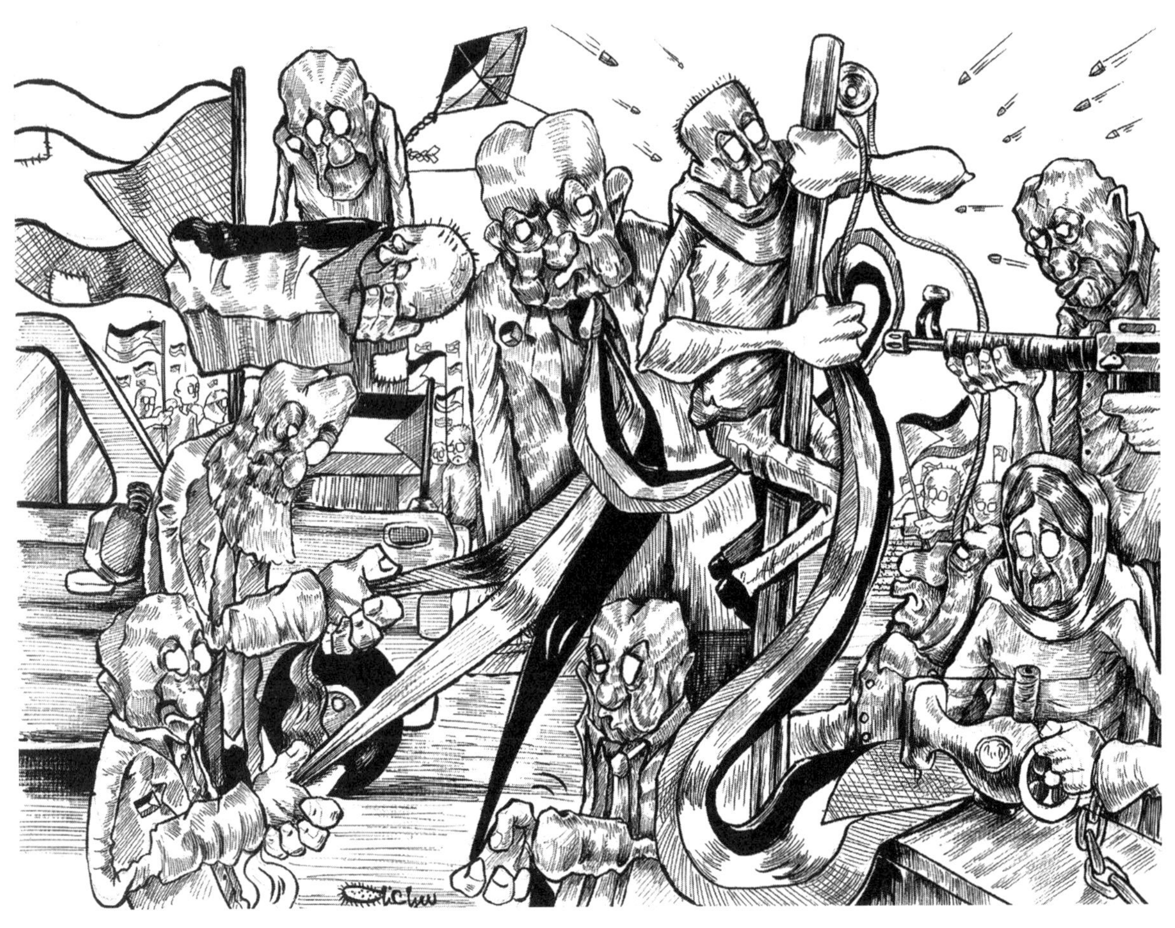

There was a time when raising the flag was an act of defiance.

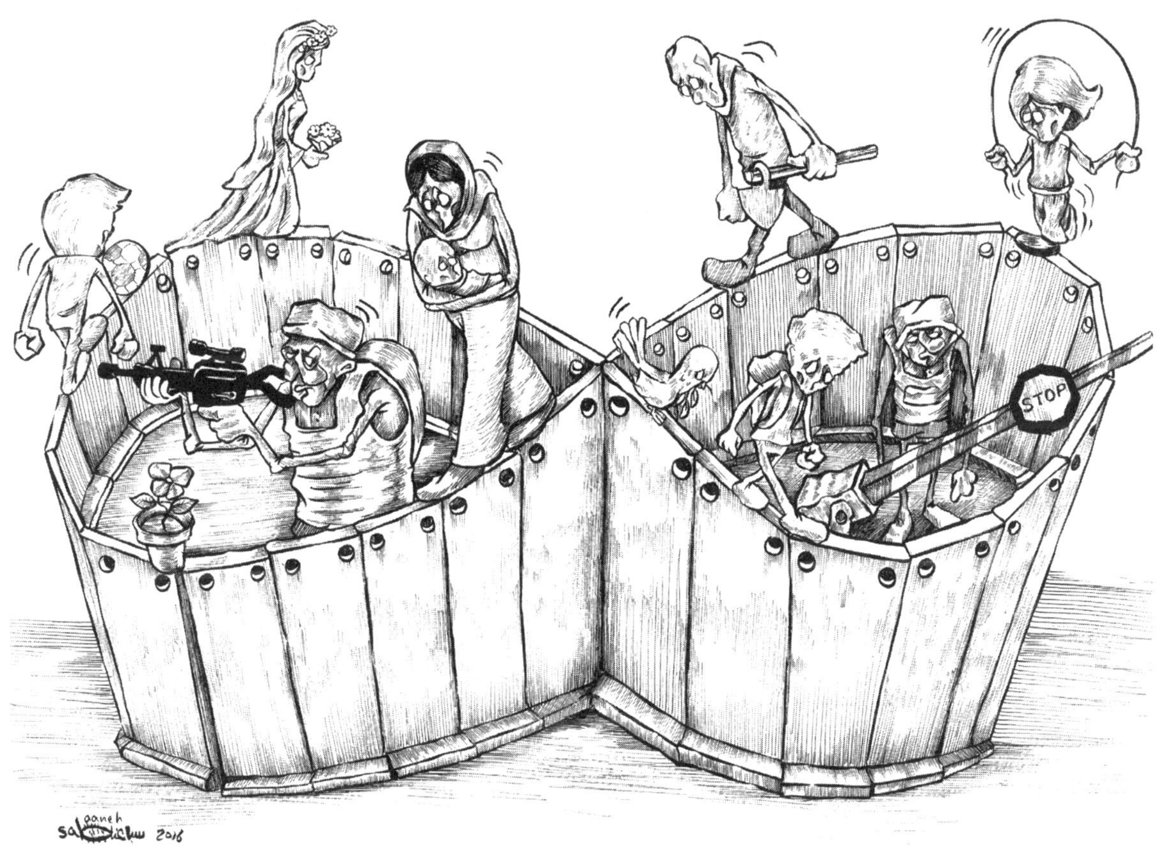

How much longer?

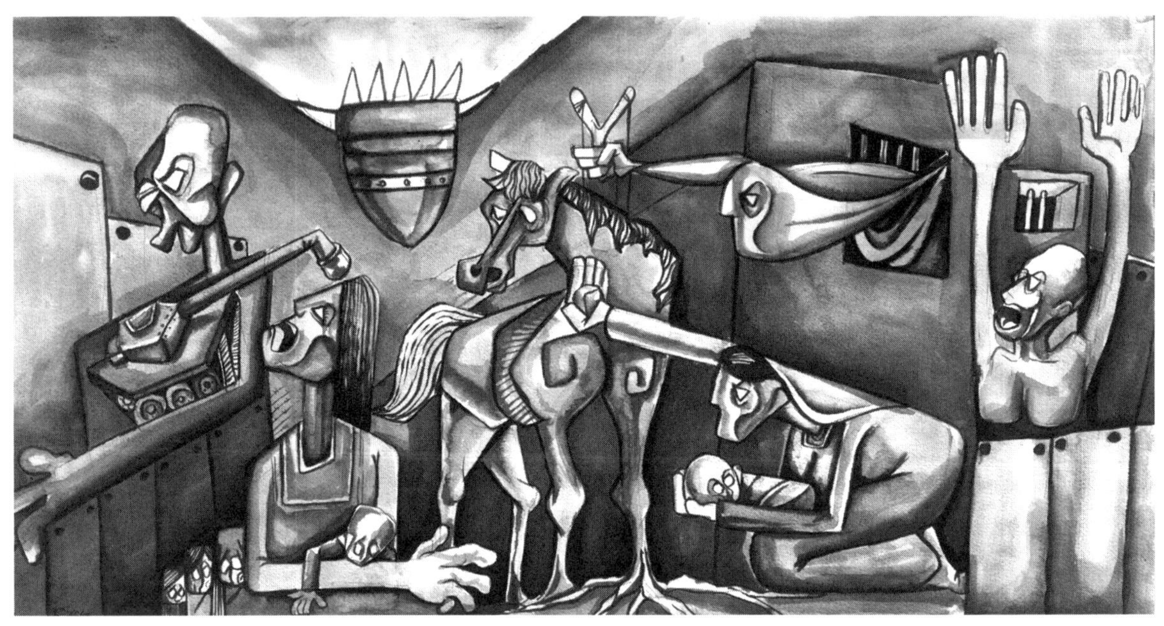

The first intifada.

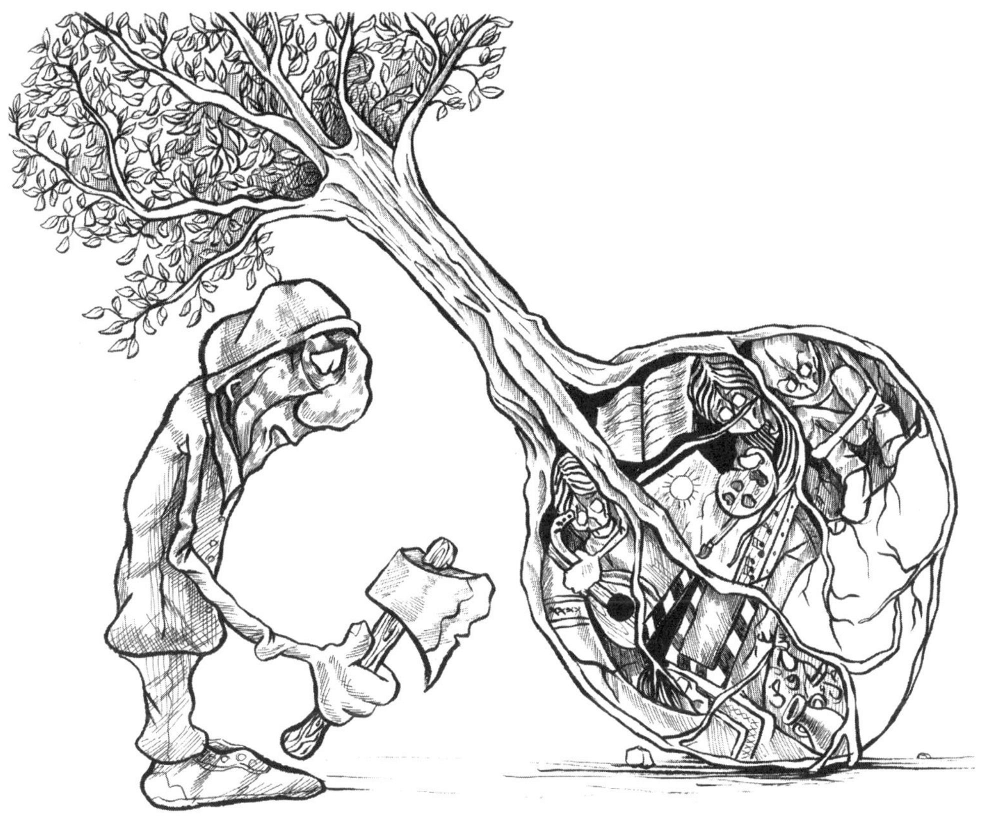

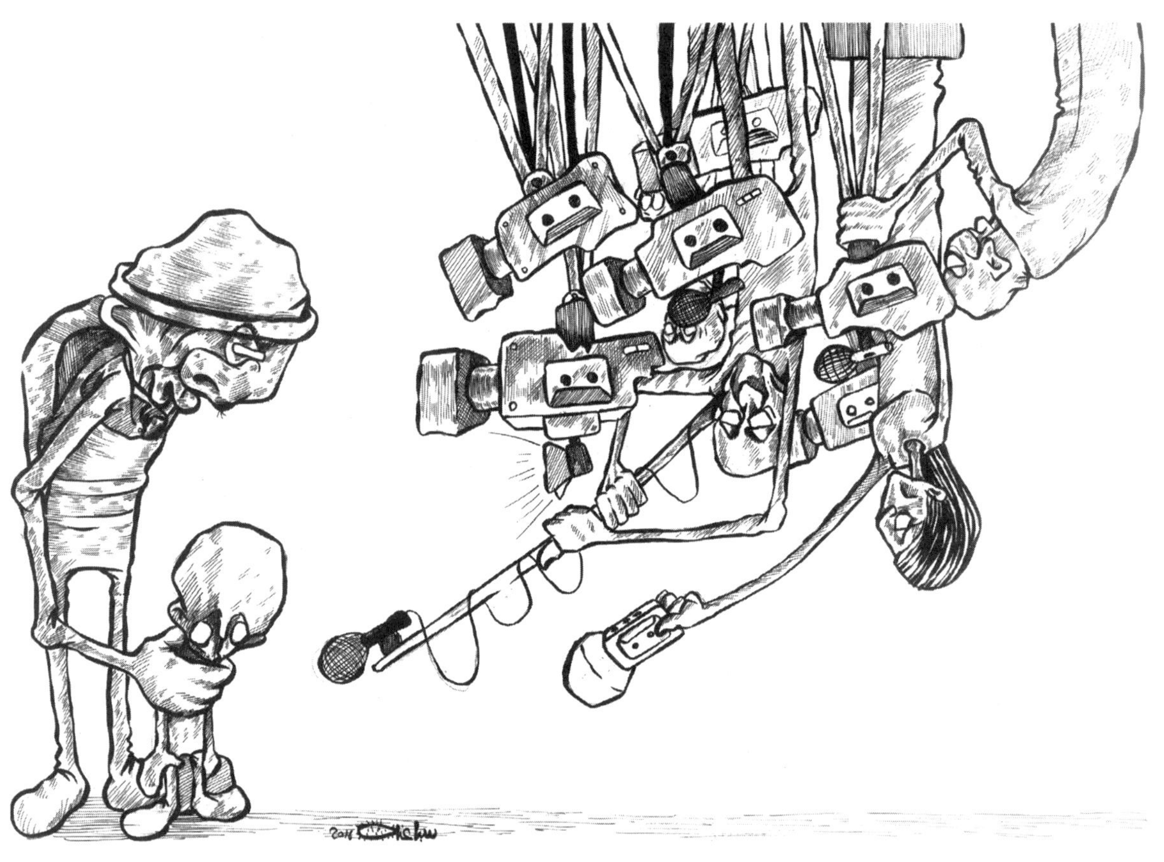

Bringing you the news.

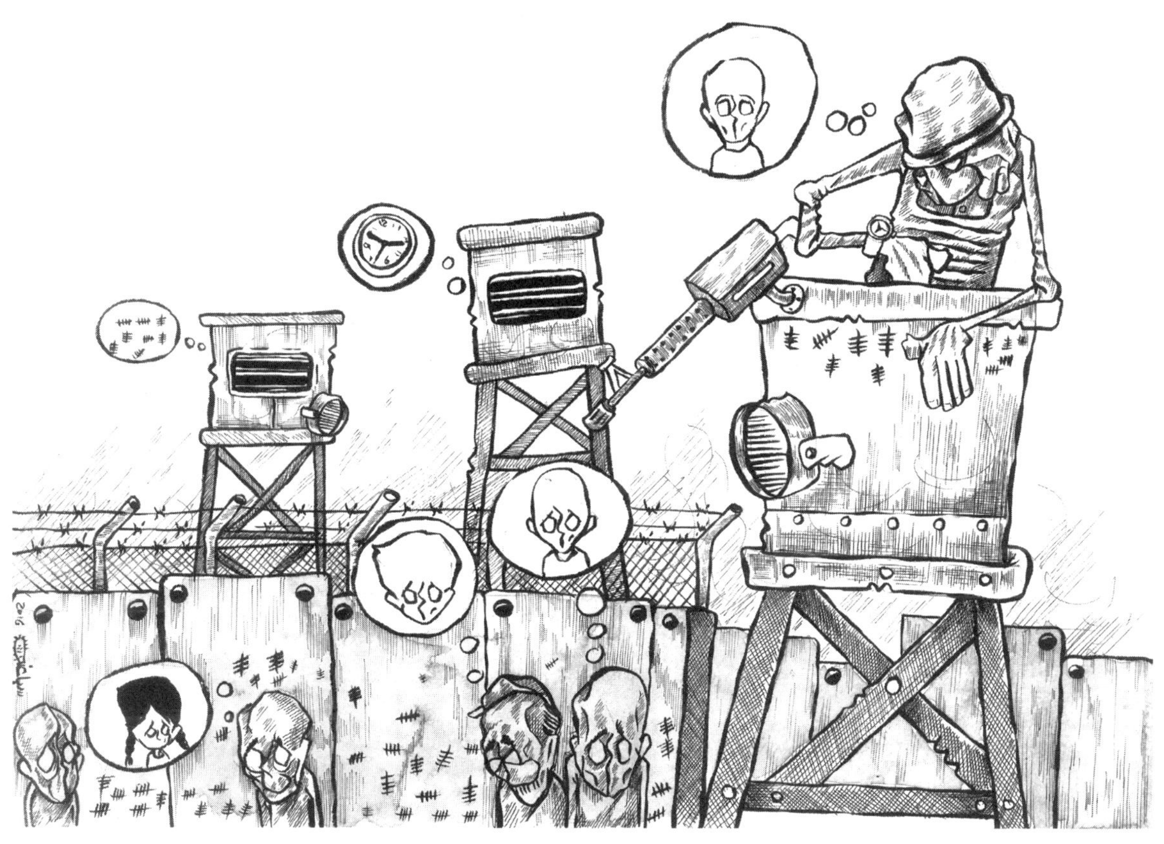

Marking time.

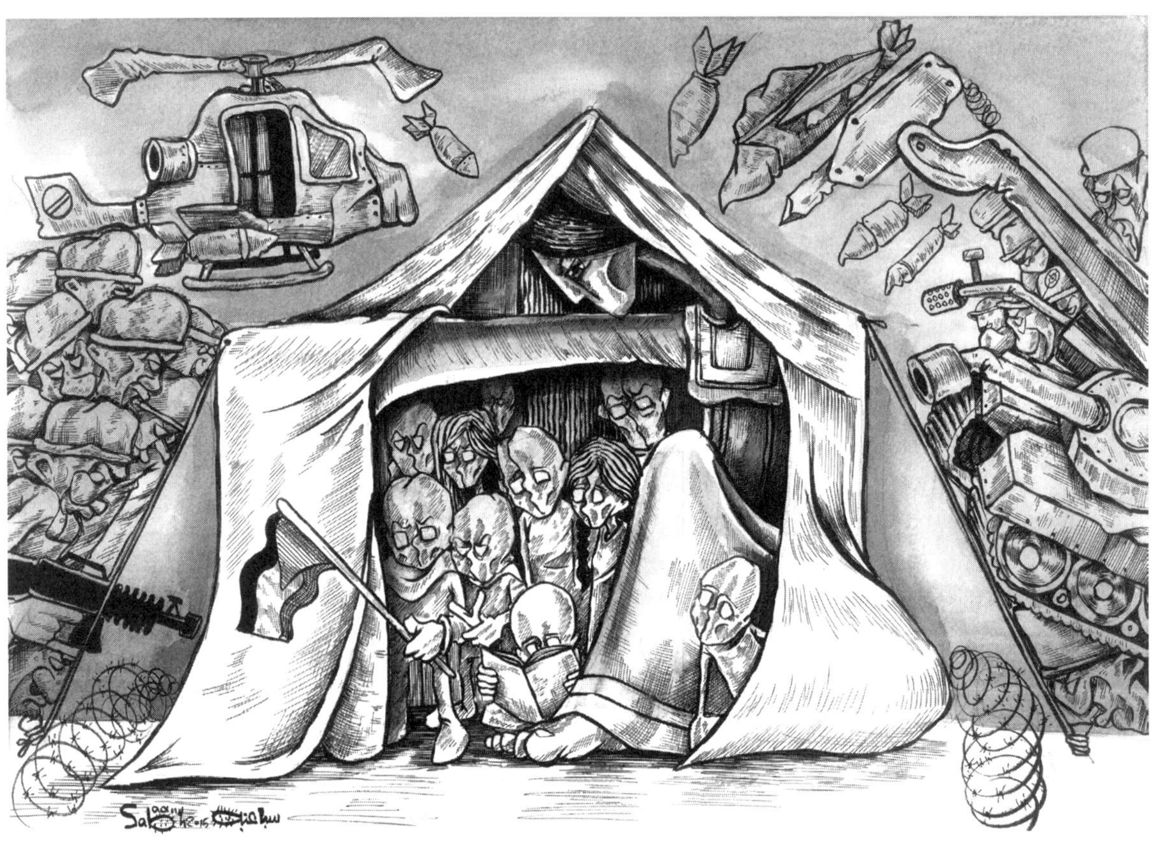

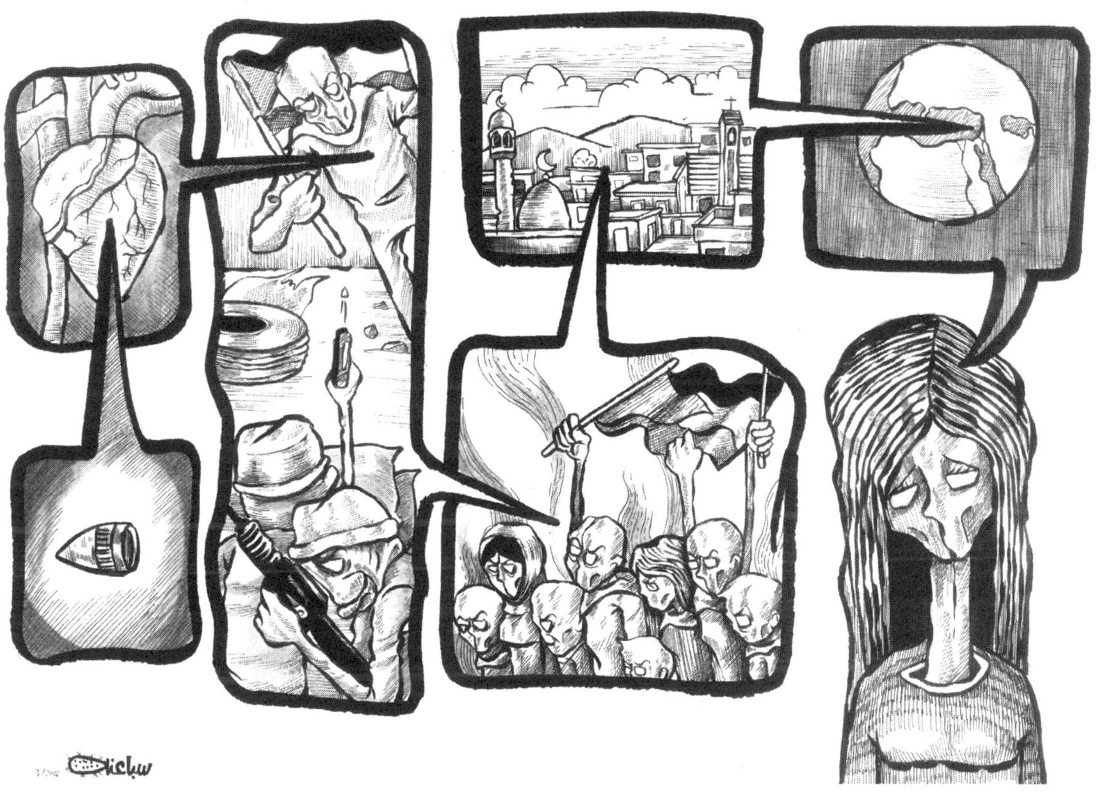

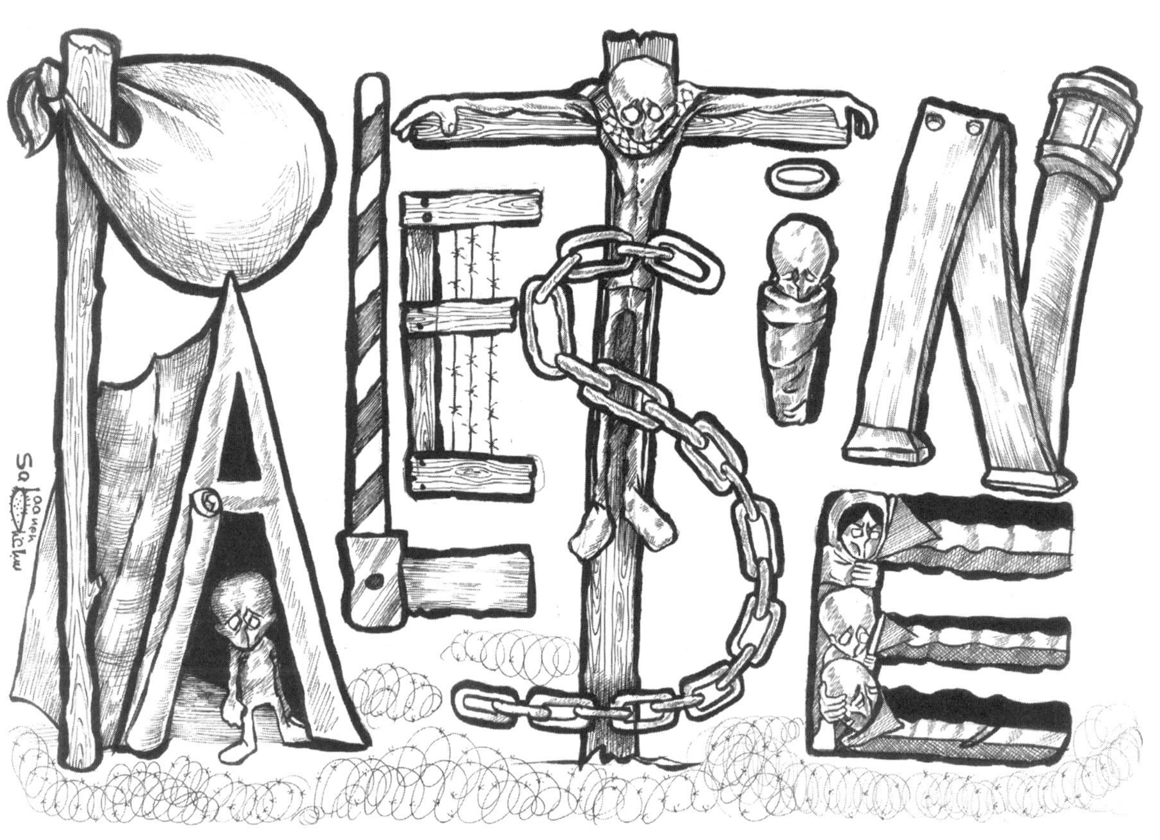

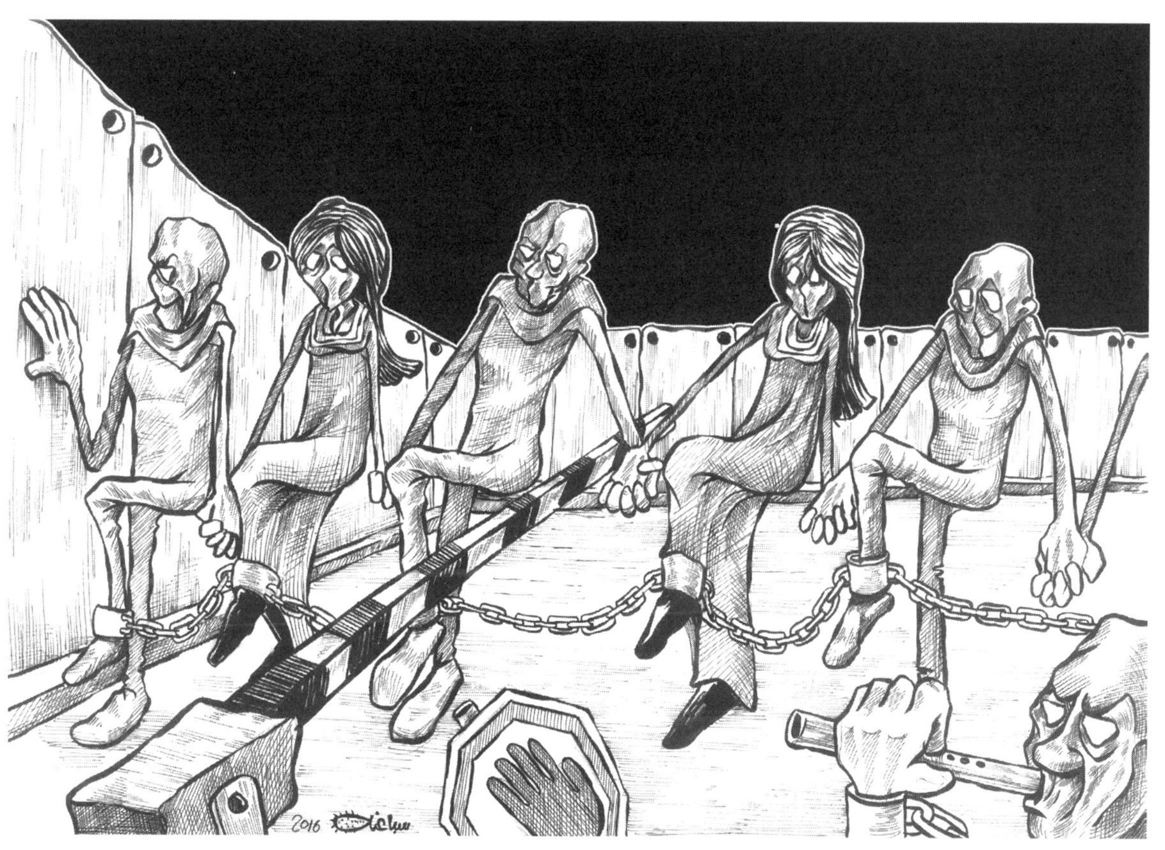

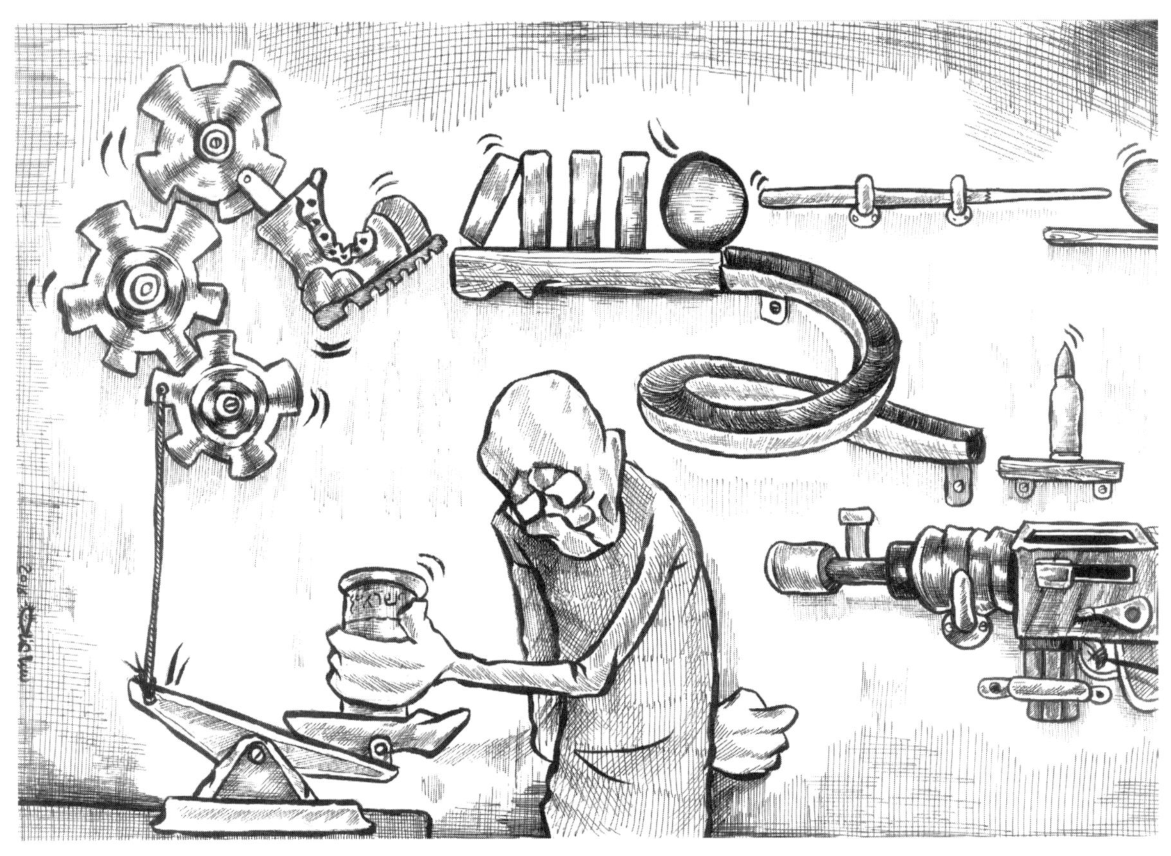

Made in Israel.

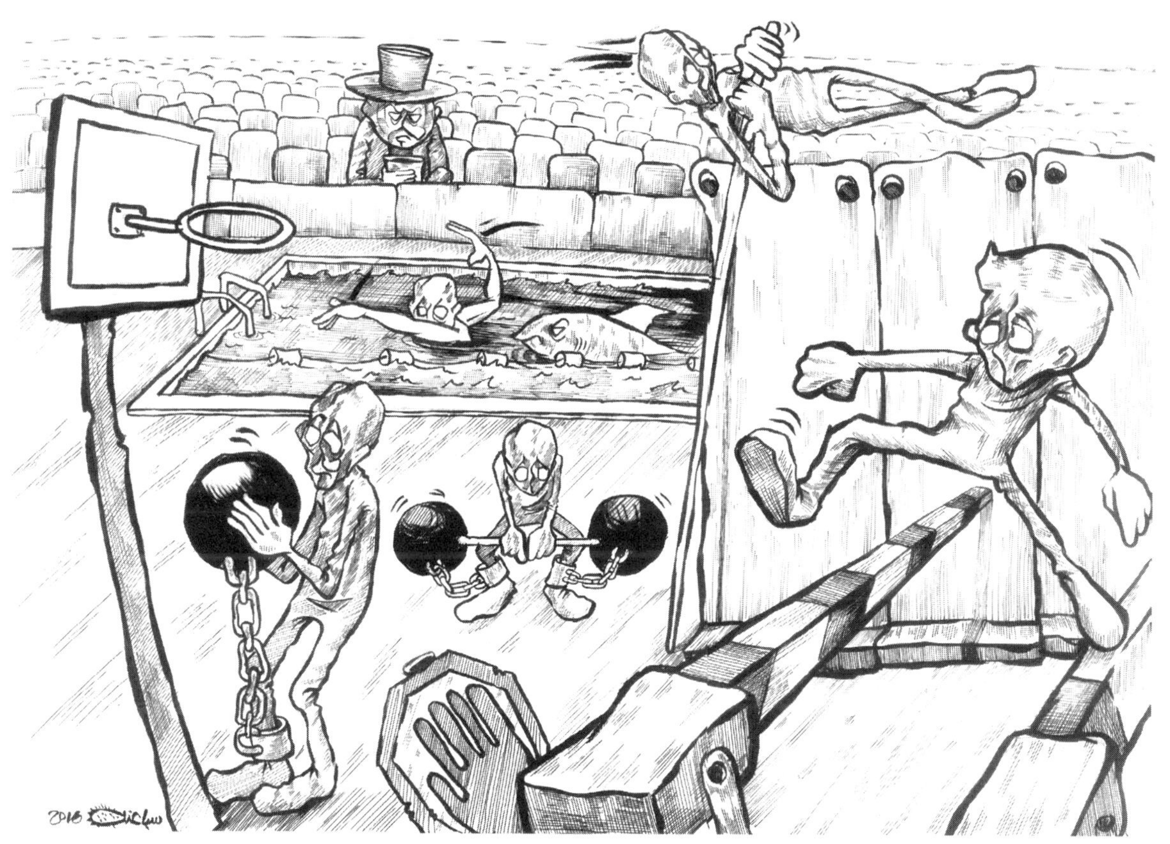

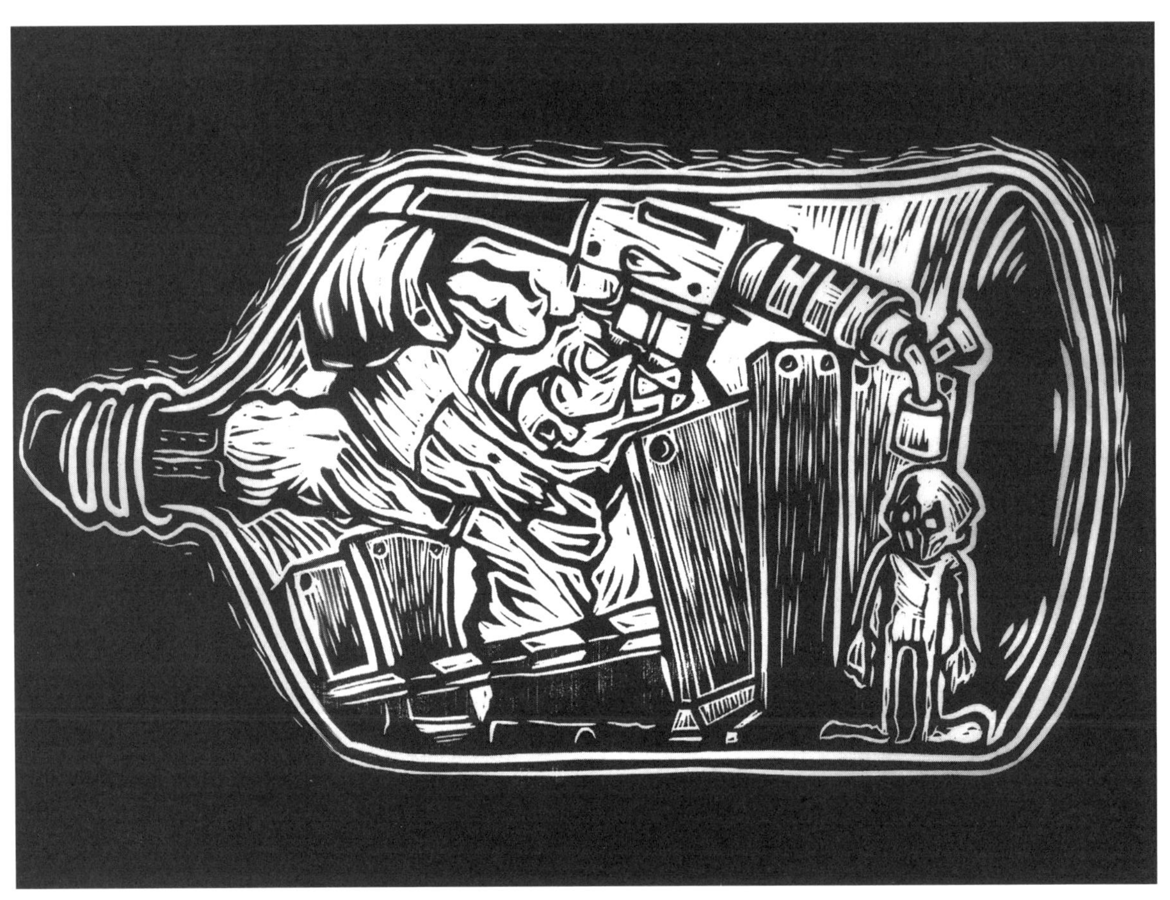

We are all hostages.

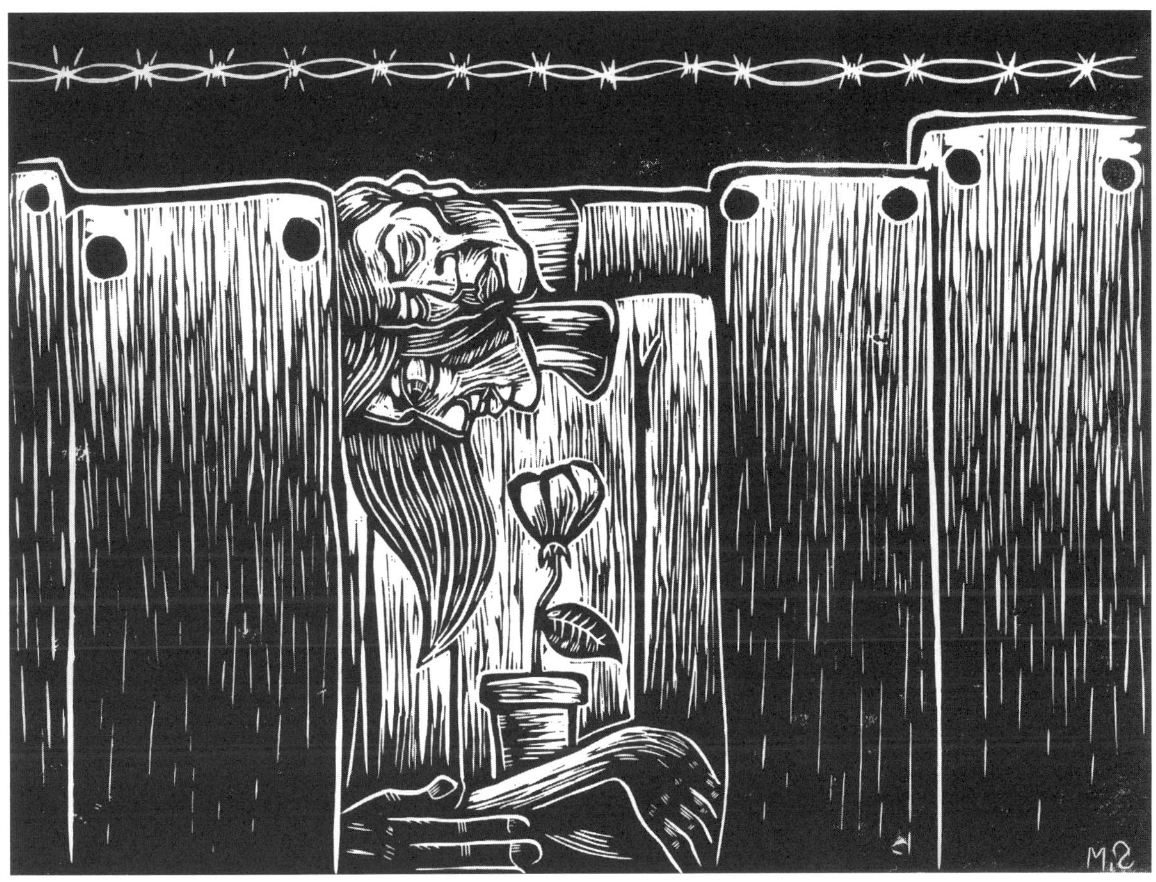

Life in spite of the siege.

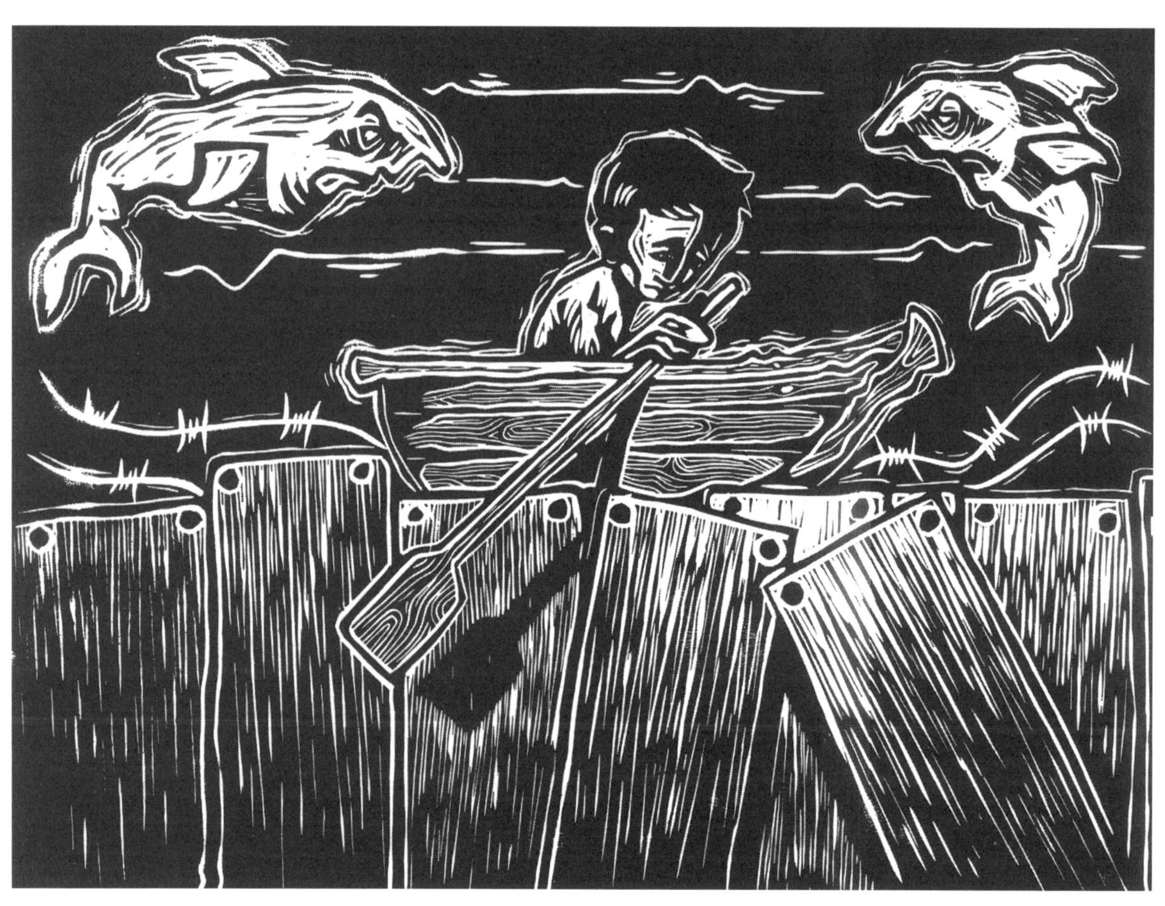

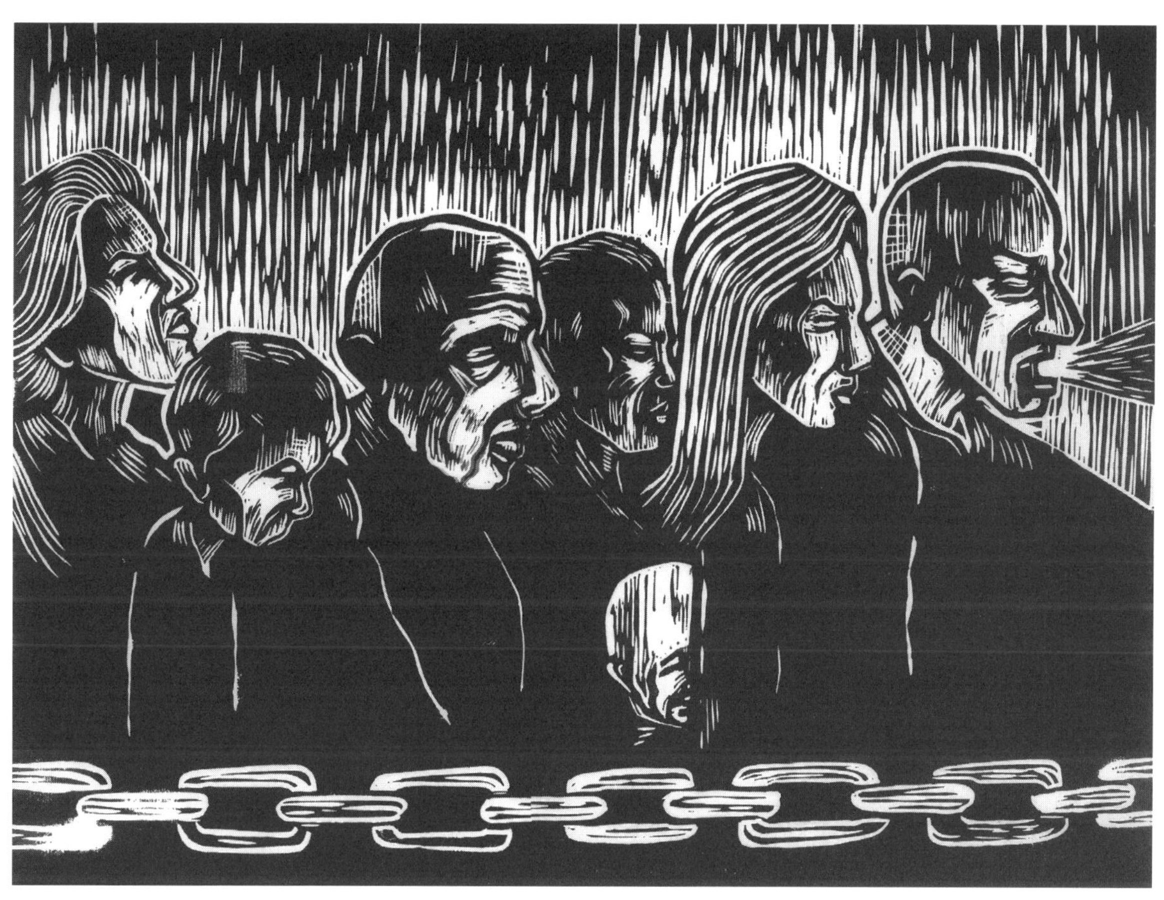

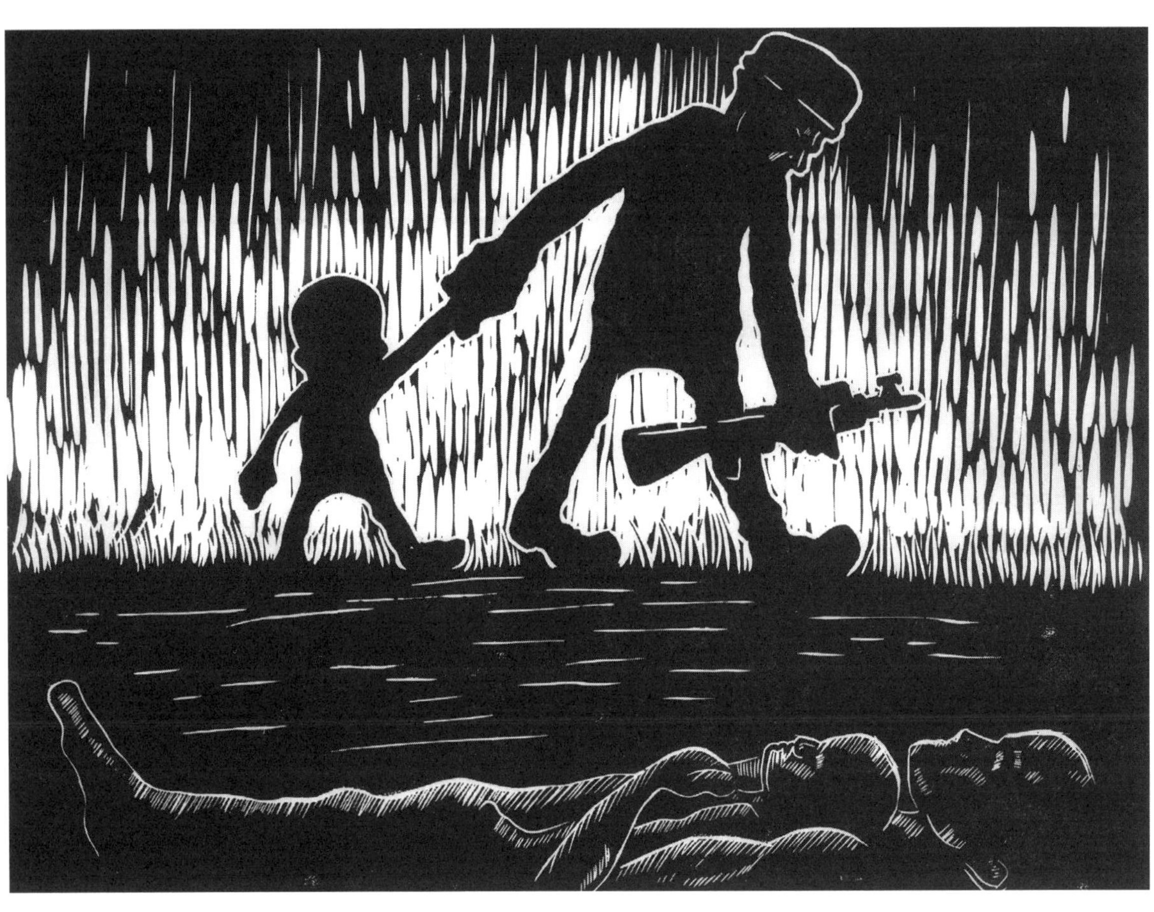

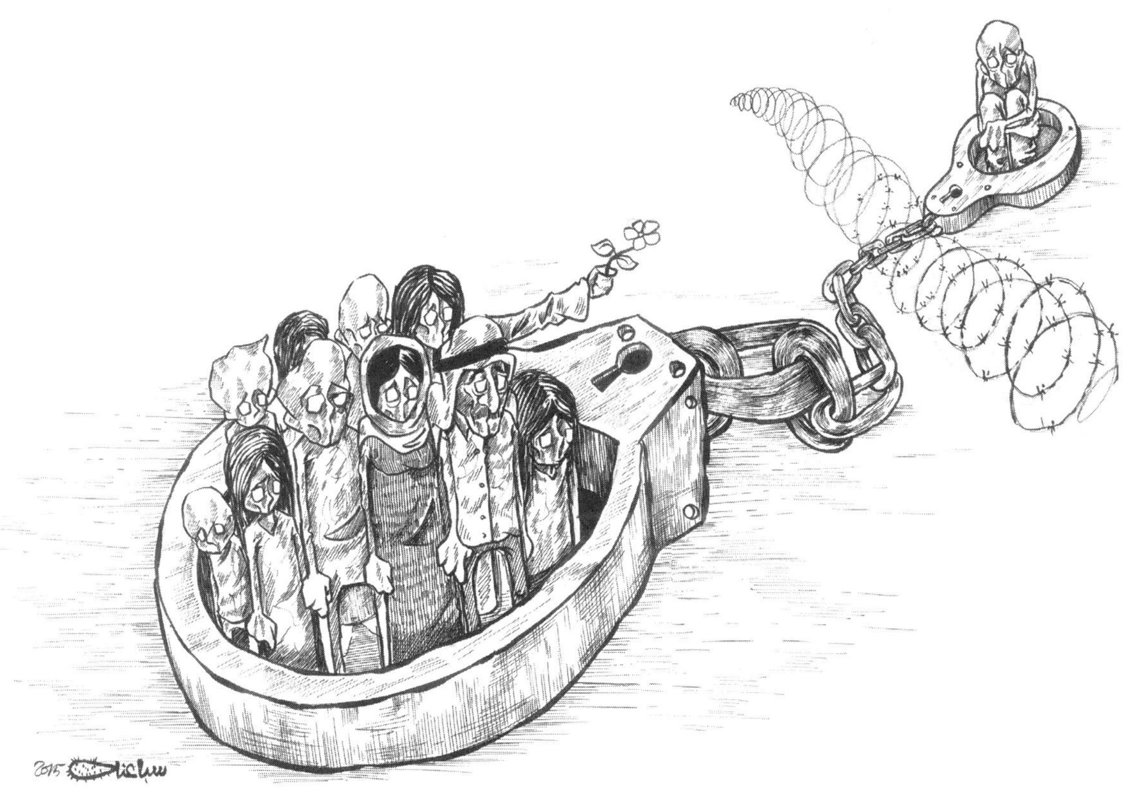

Families of political prisoners are prisoners too.

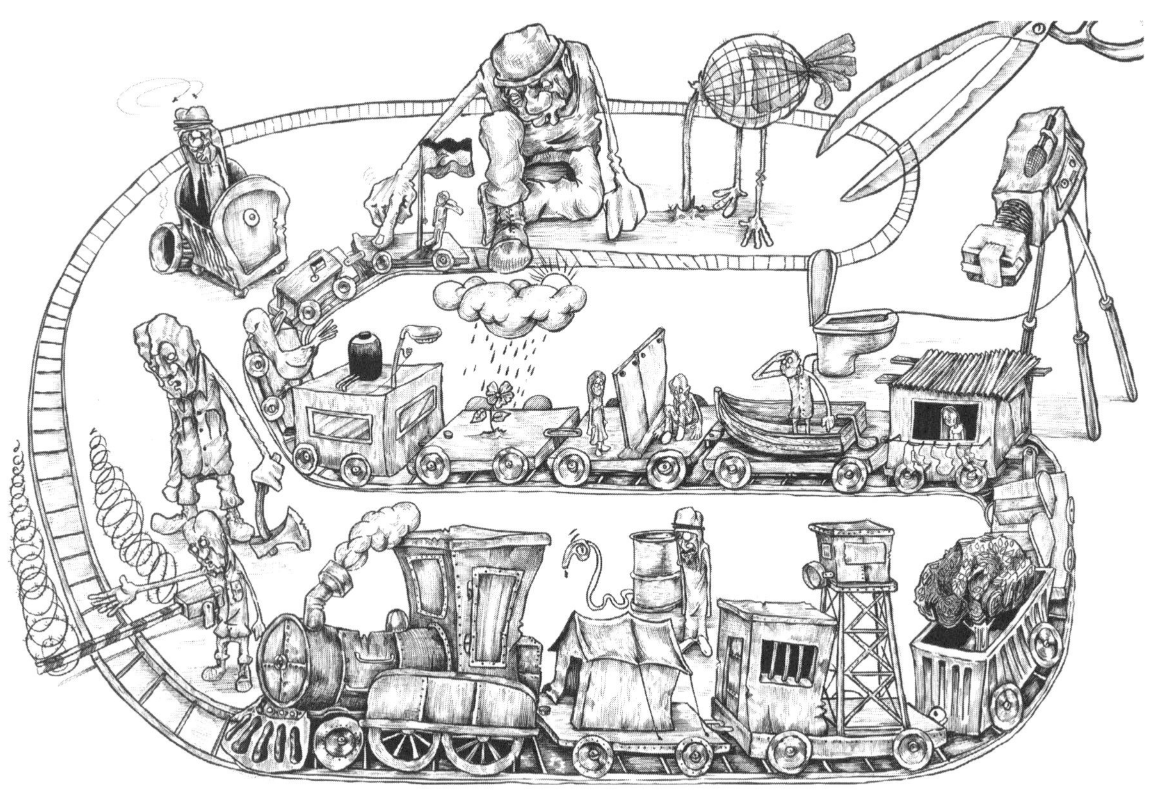

A Palestinian life.

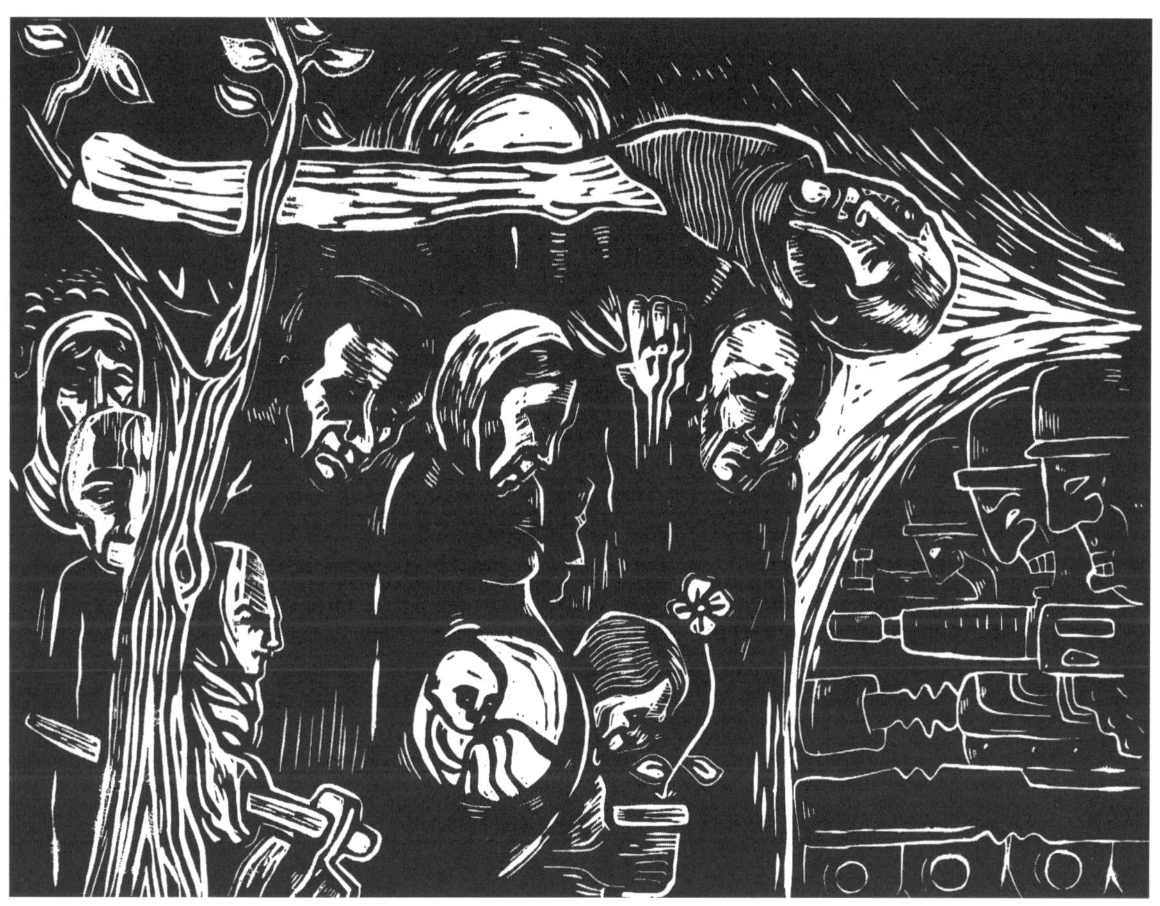

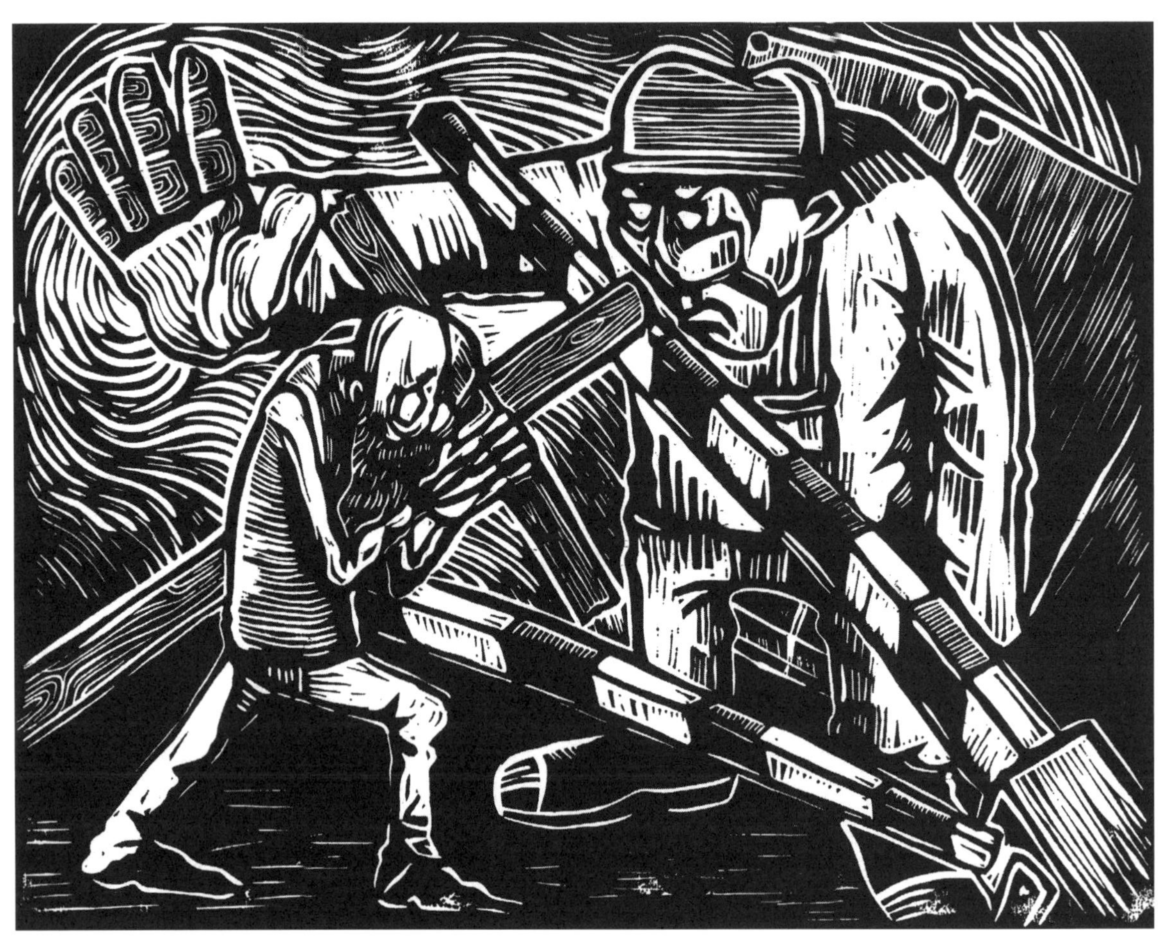

Via Dolorosa.

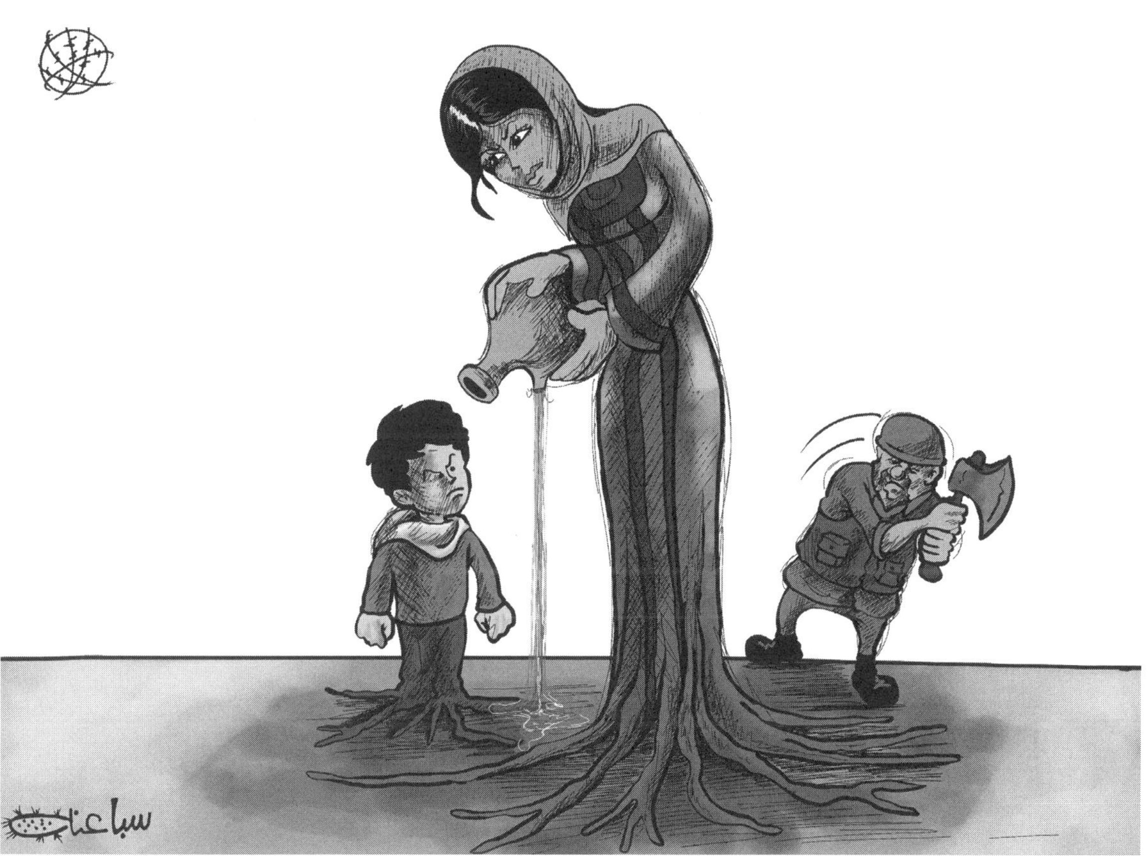
سباعنة

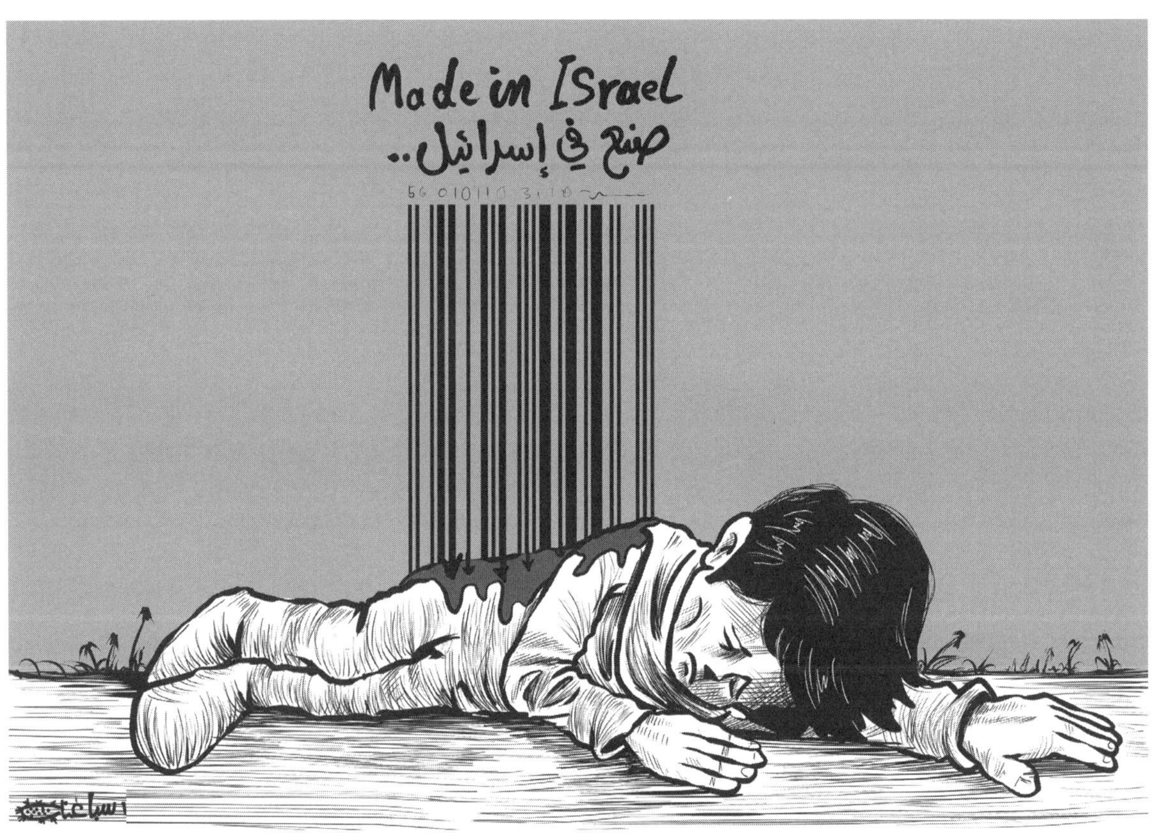
Made in Israel
صنع في إسرائيل..

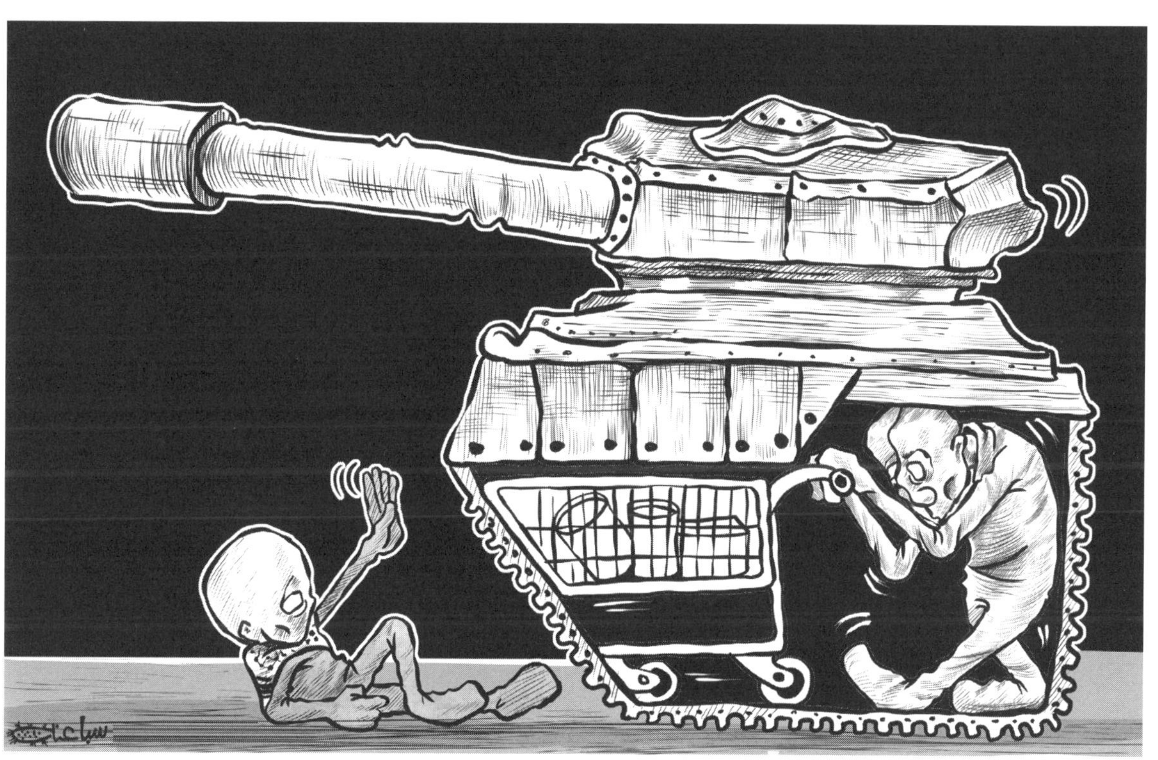

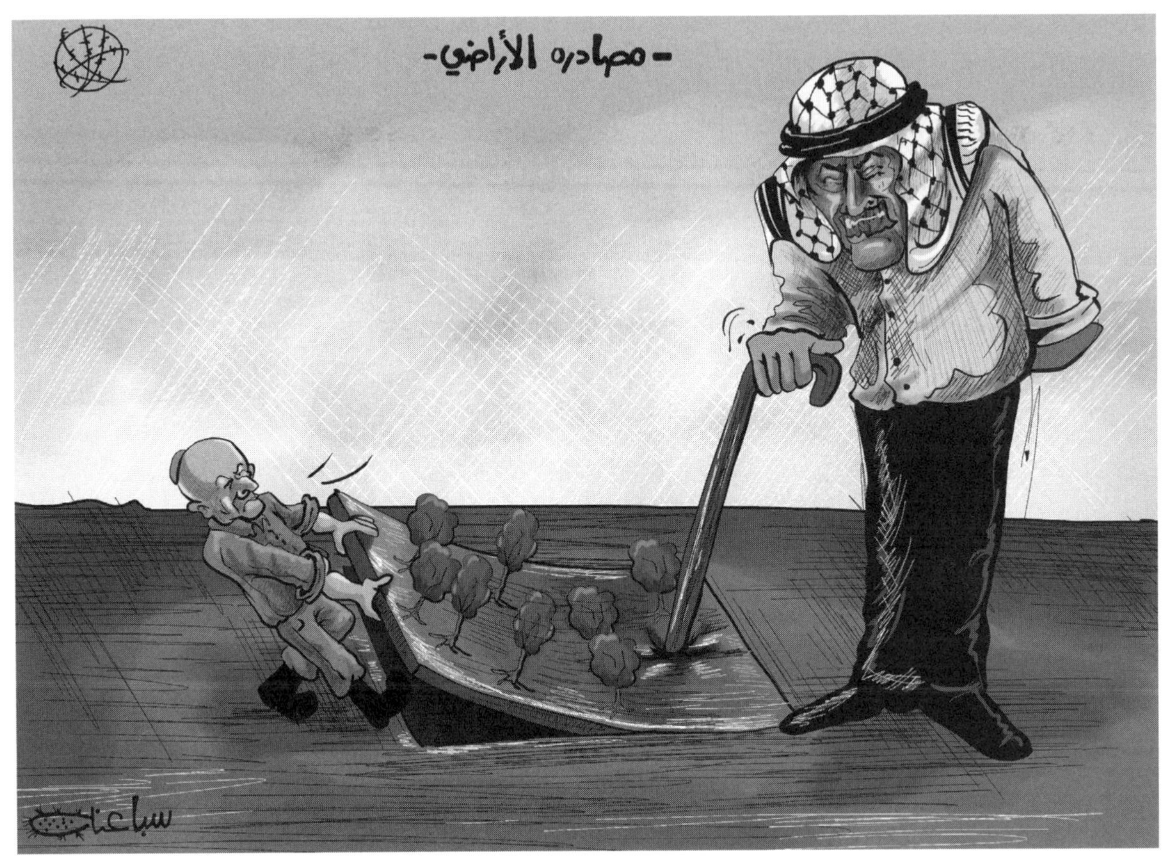

It's not yours to claim.

3

PALESTINE AND THE WORLD

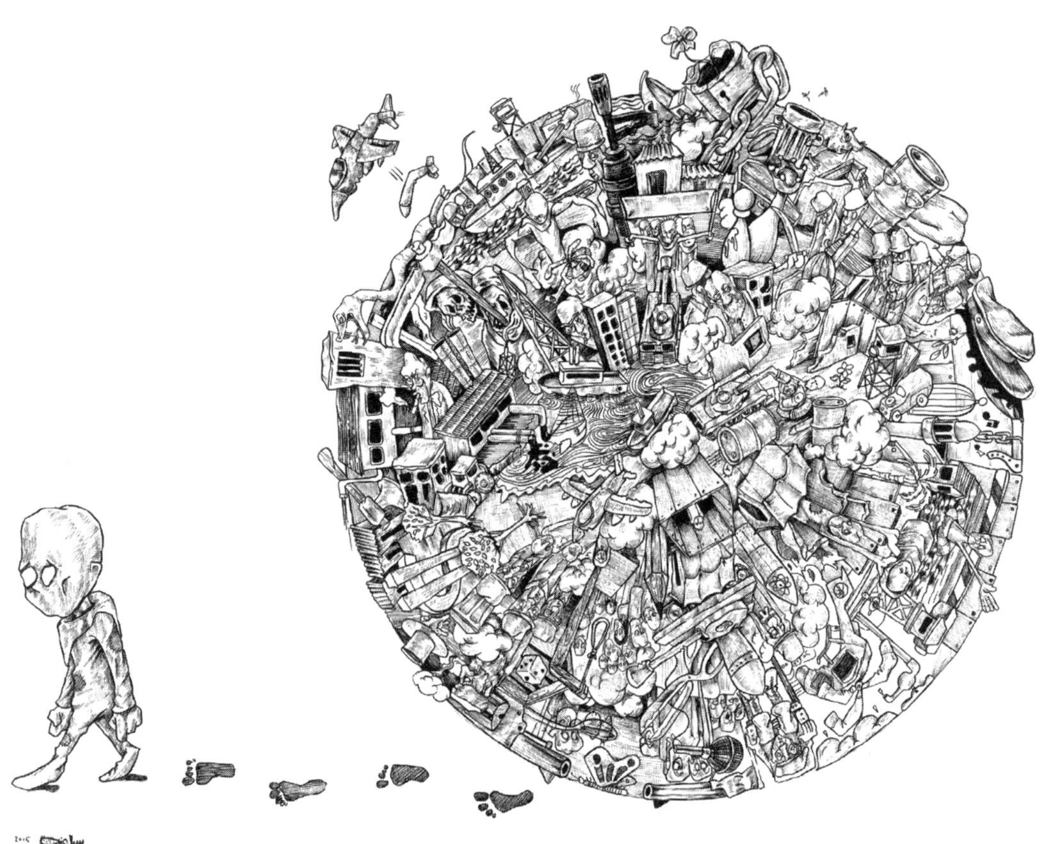

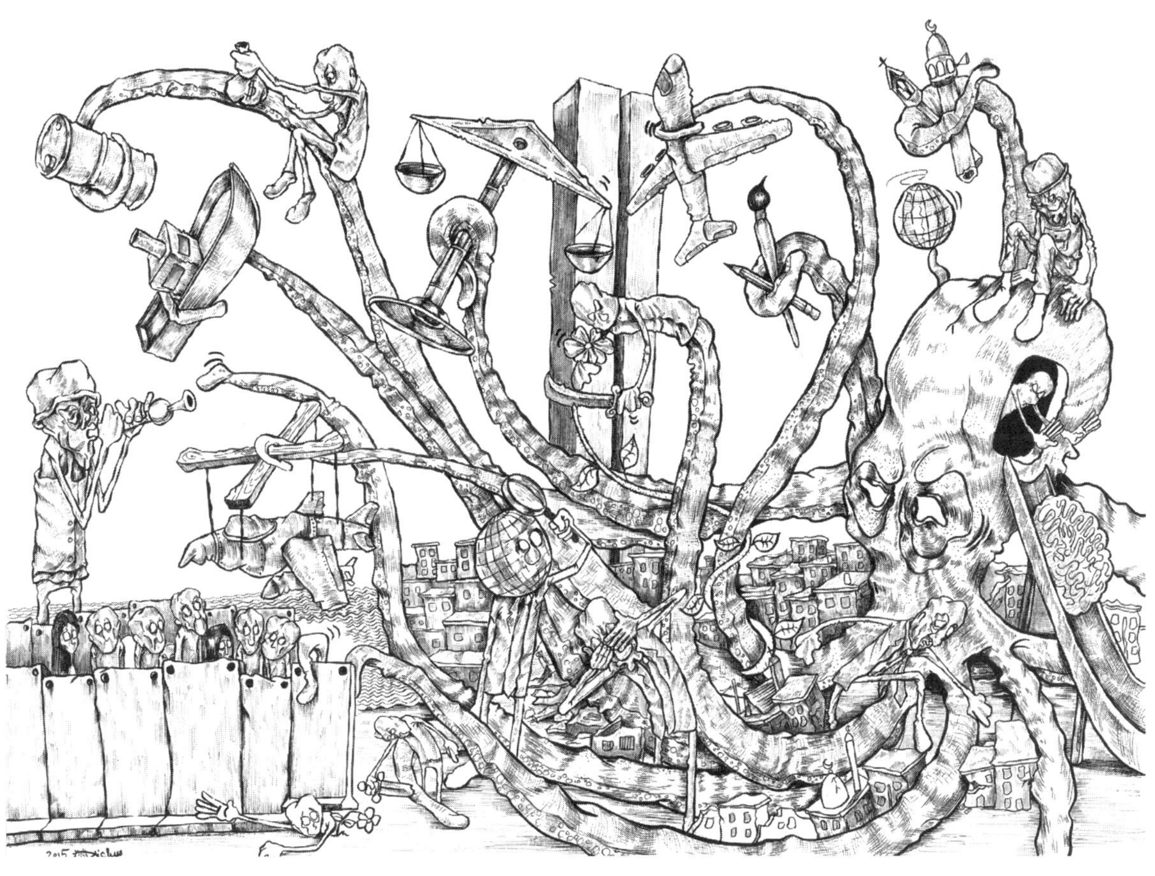

The iron grip of global forces.

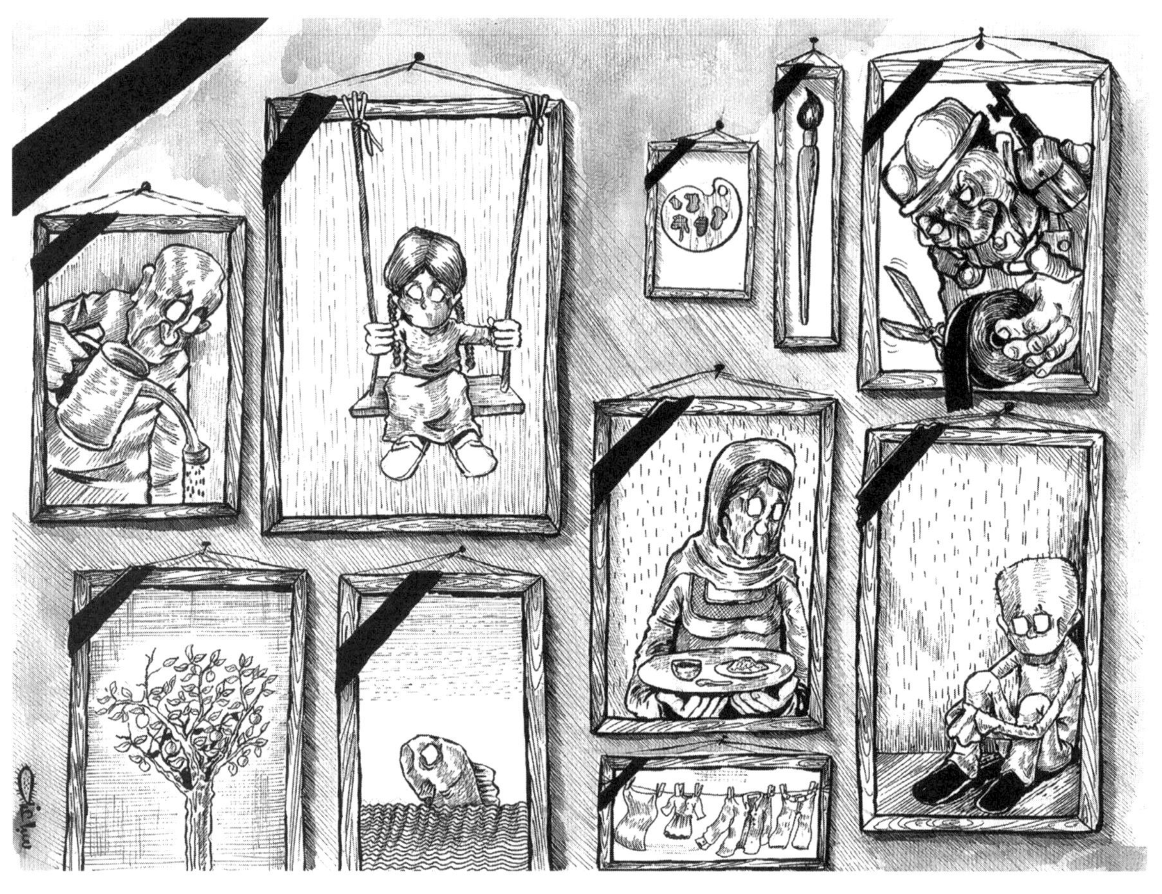

Family photos.

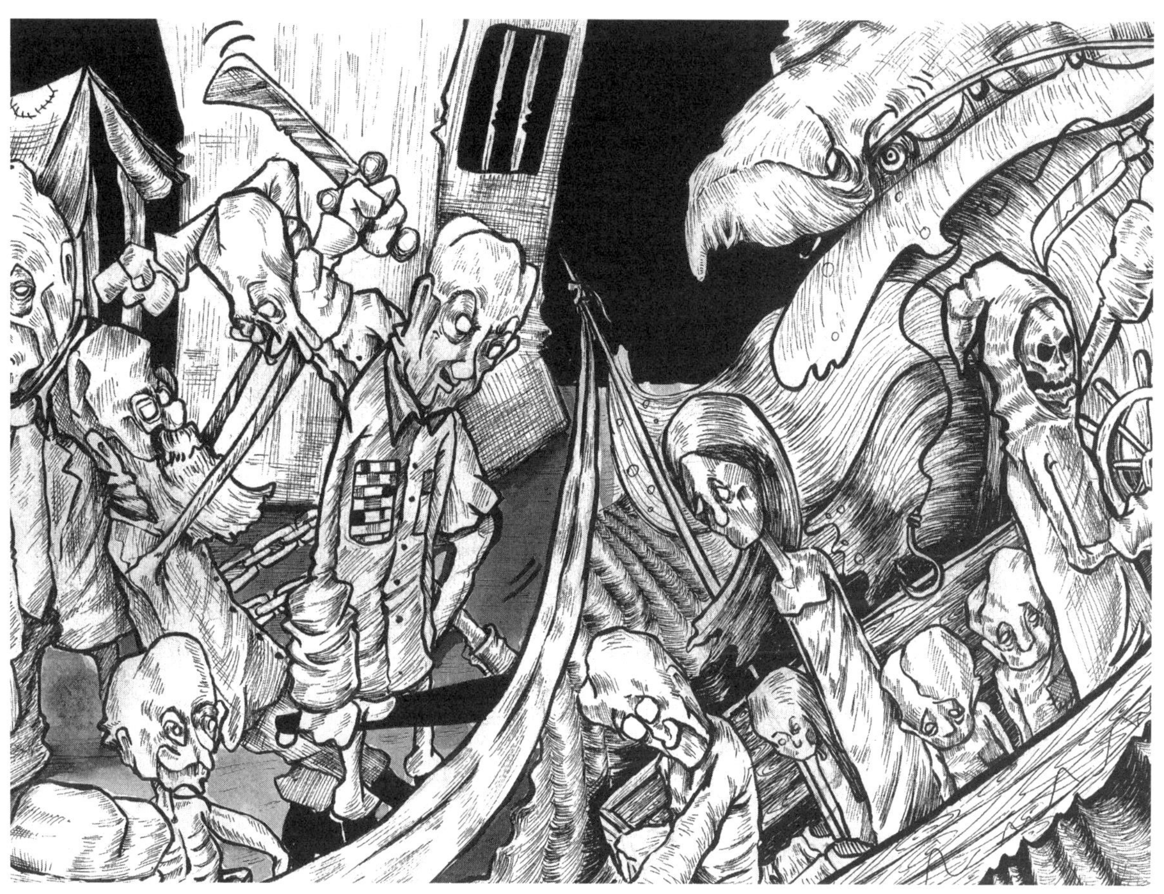

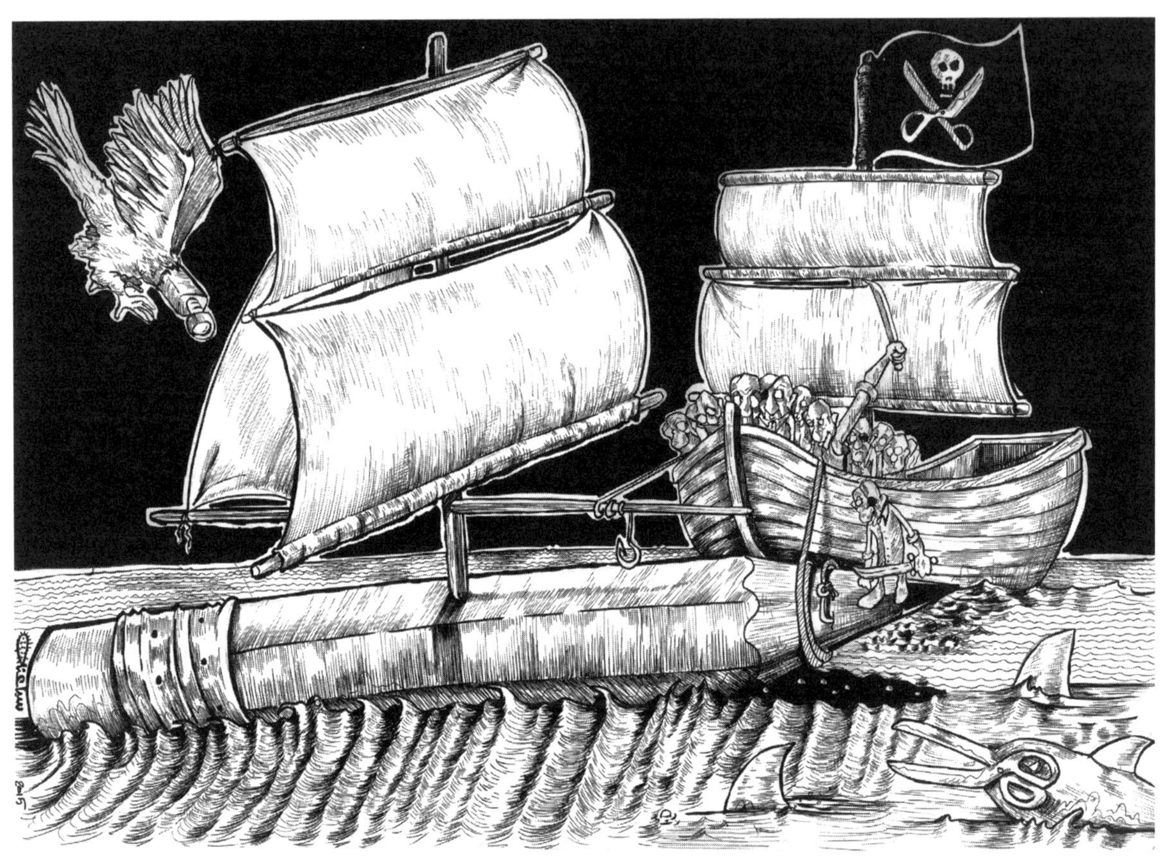

In search of freedom of expression.

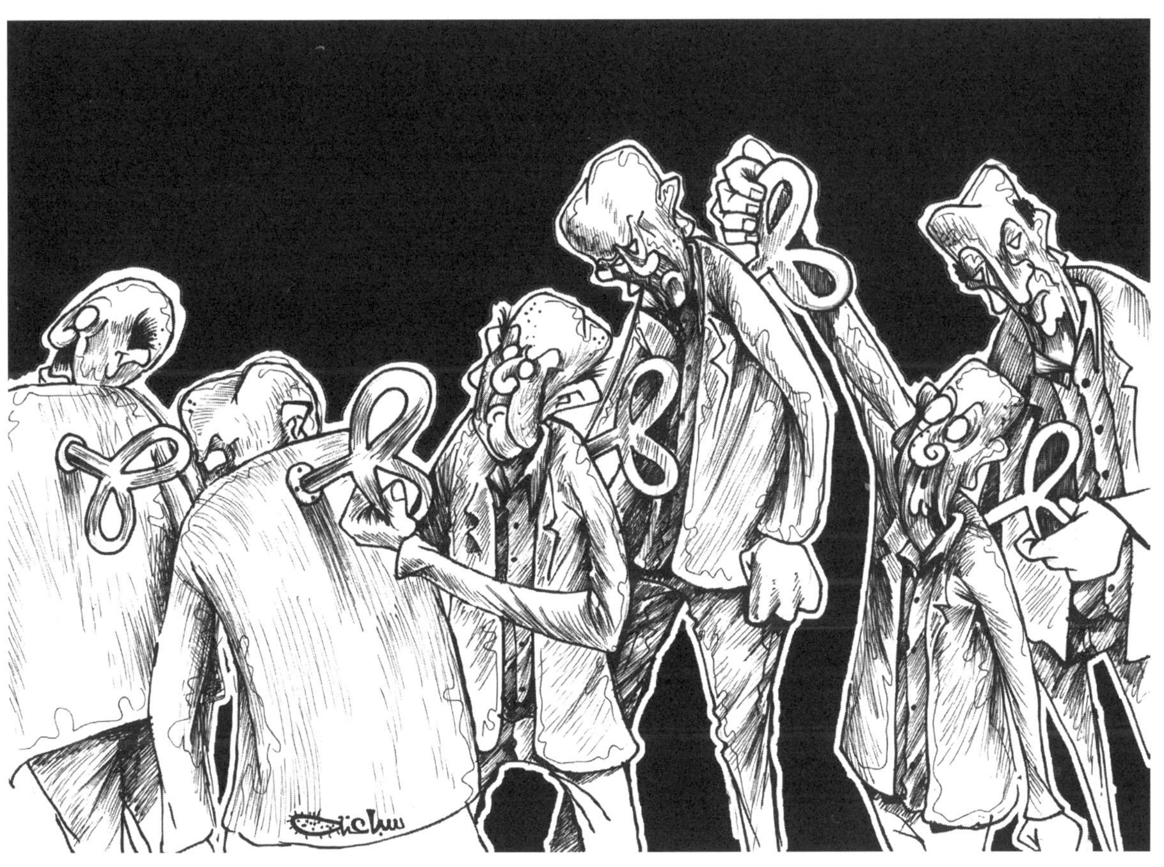

Shared interests and functional politics.

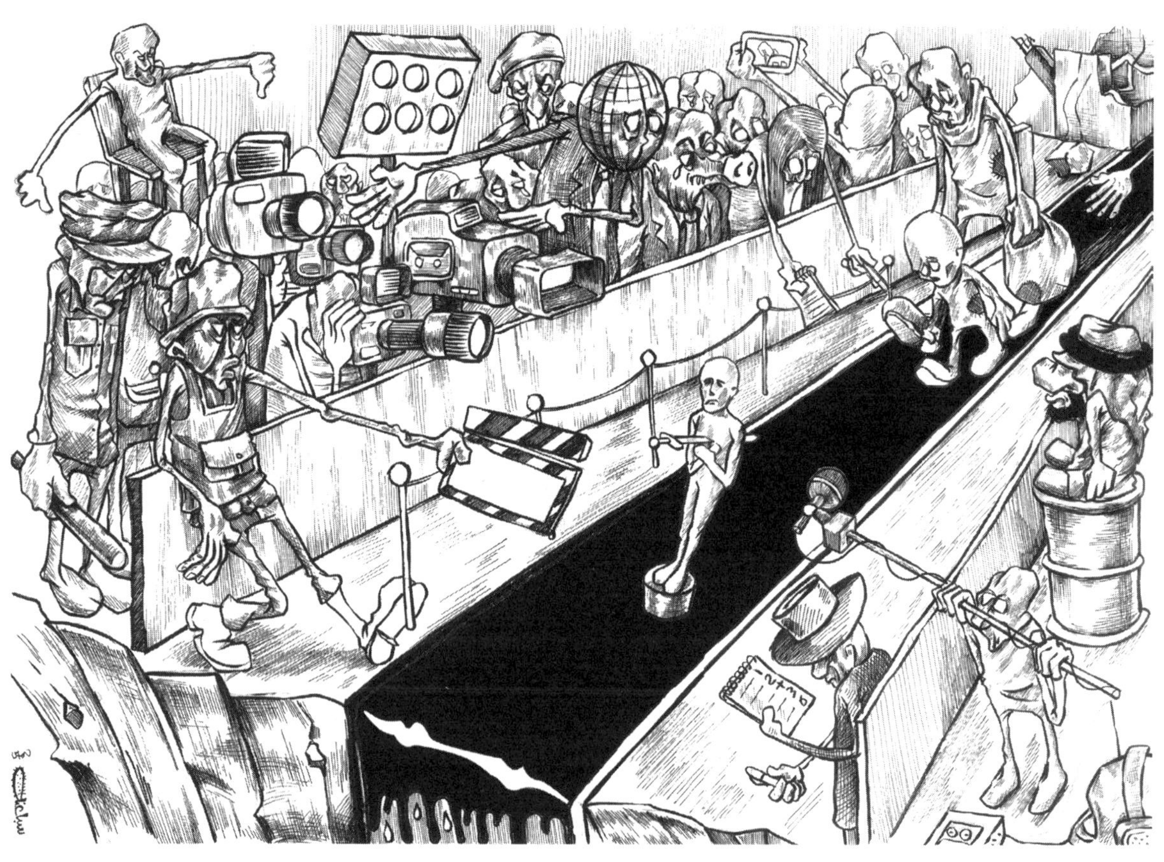

In this race there are no winners.

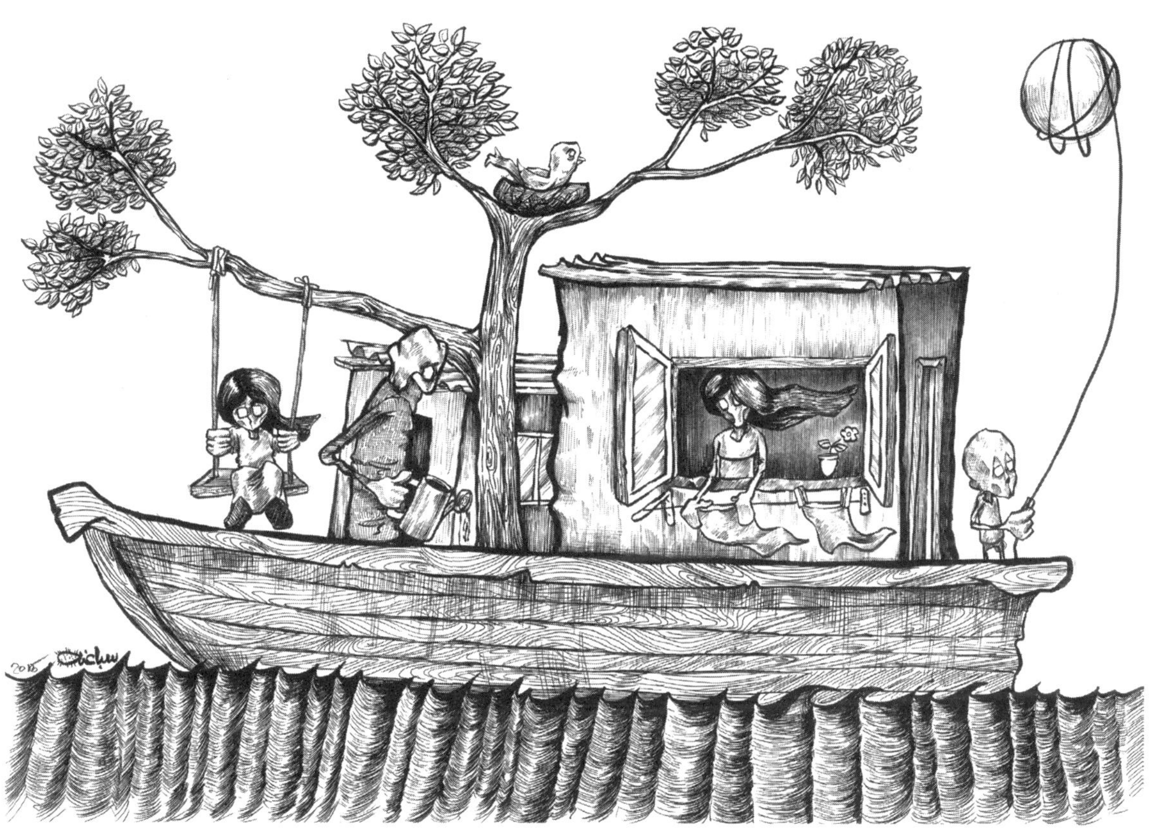

In search of a normal life.

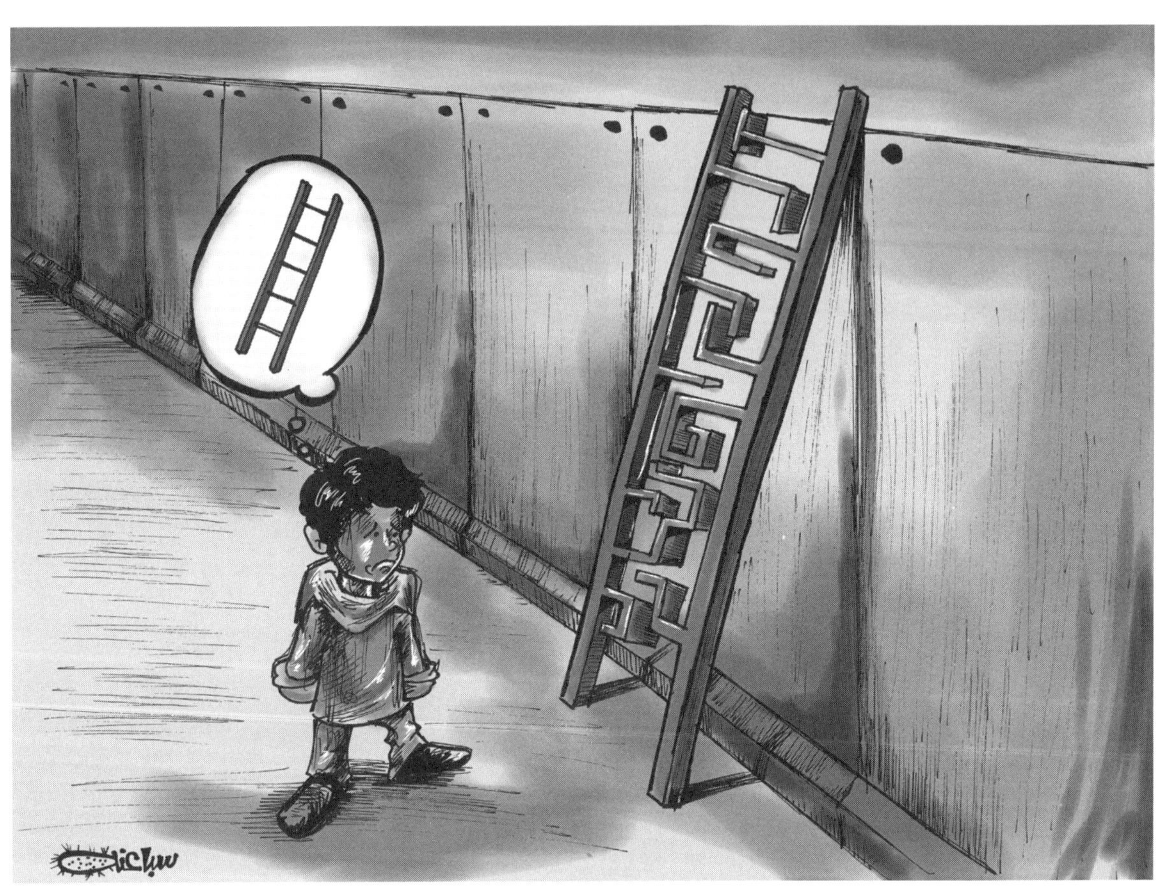

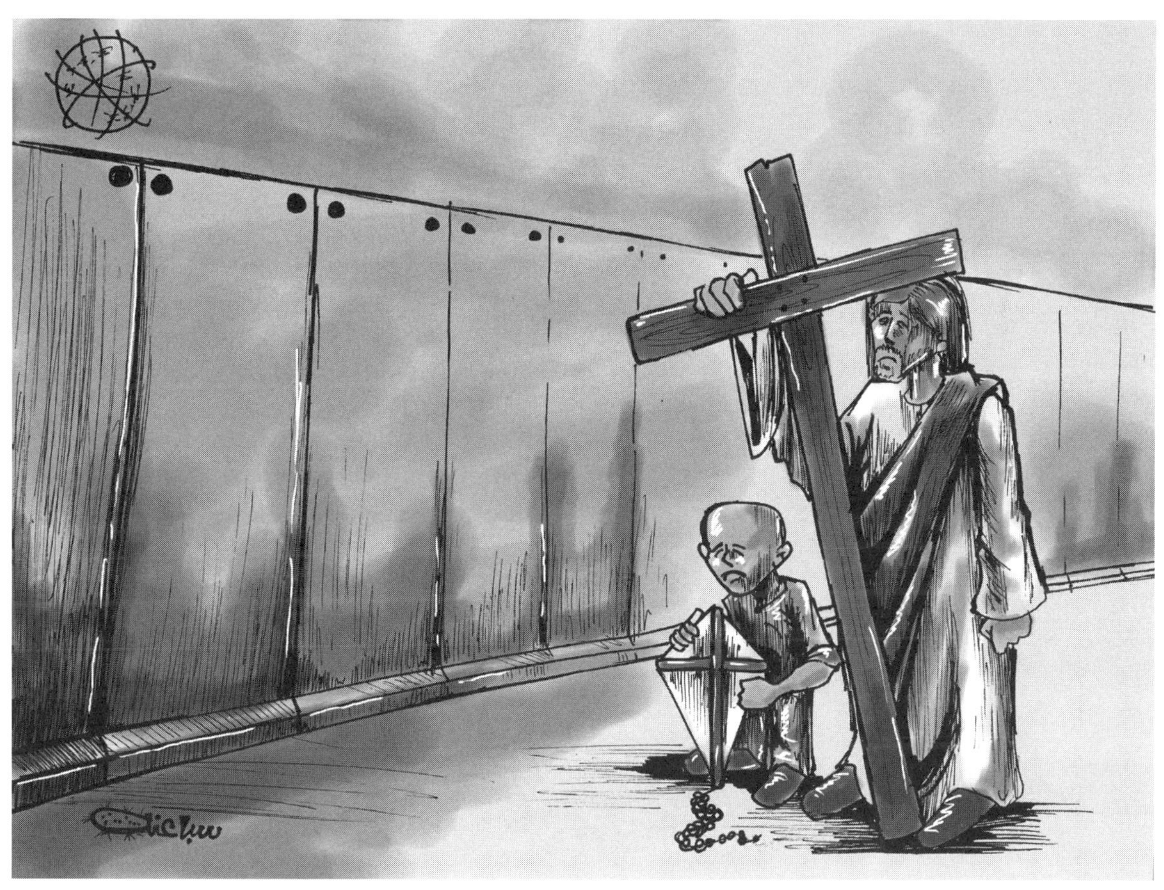

Every age has a prophet.

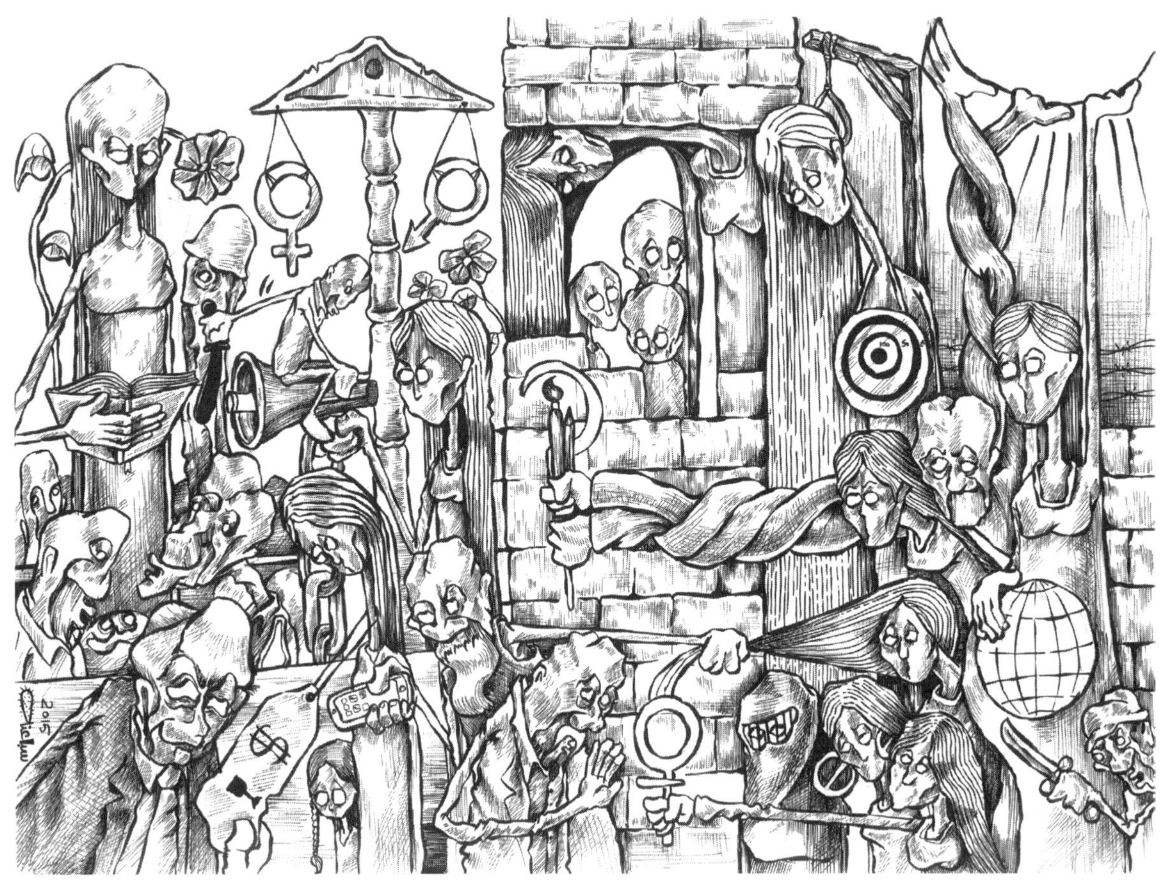

Status of women.

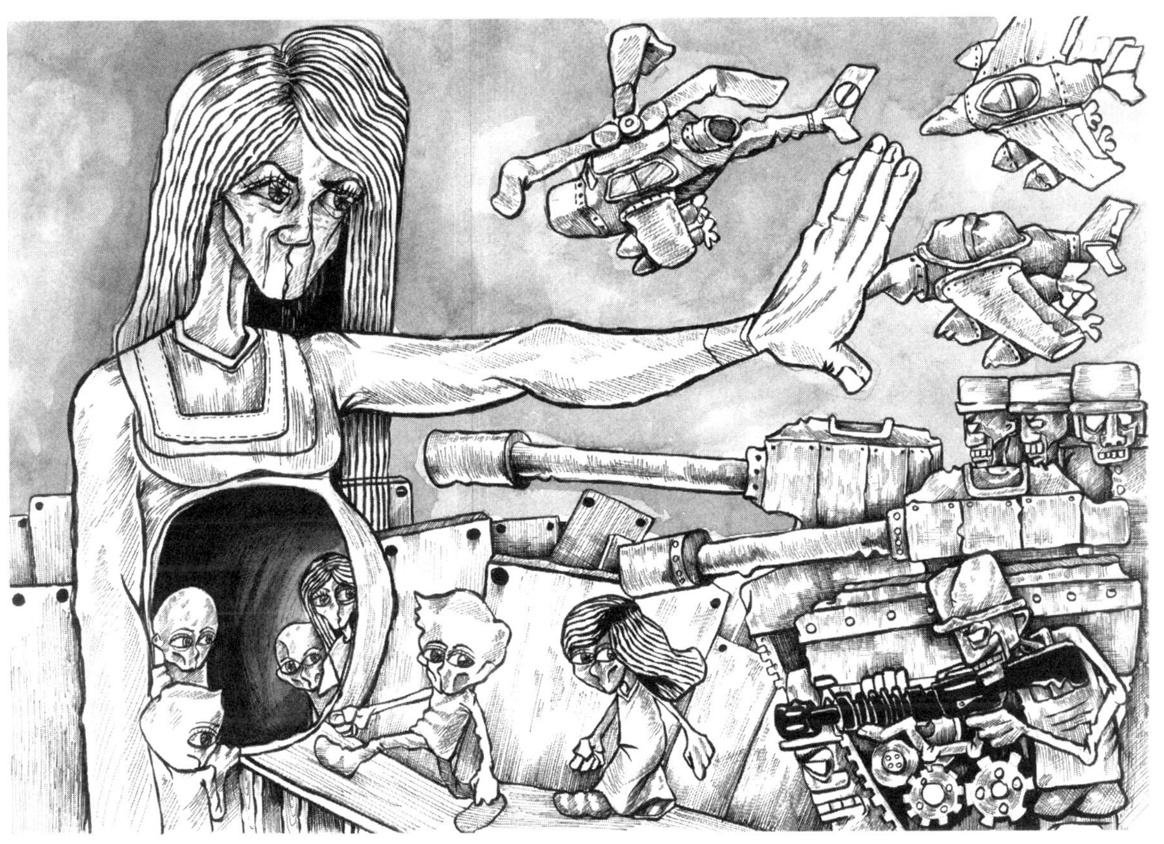

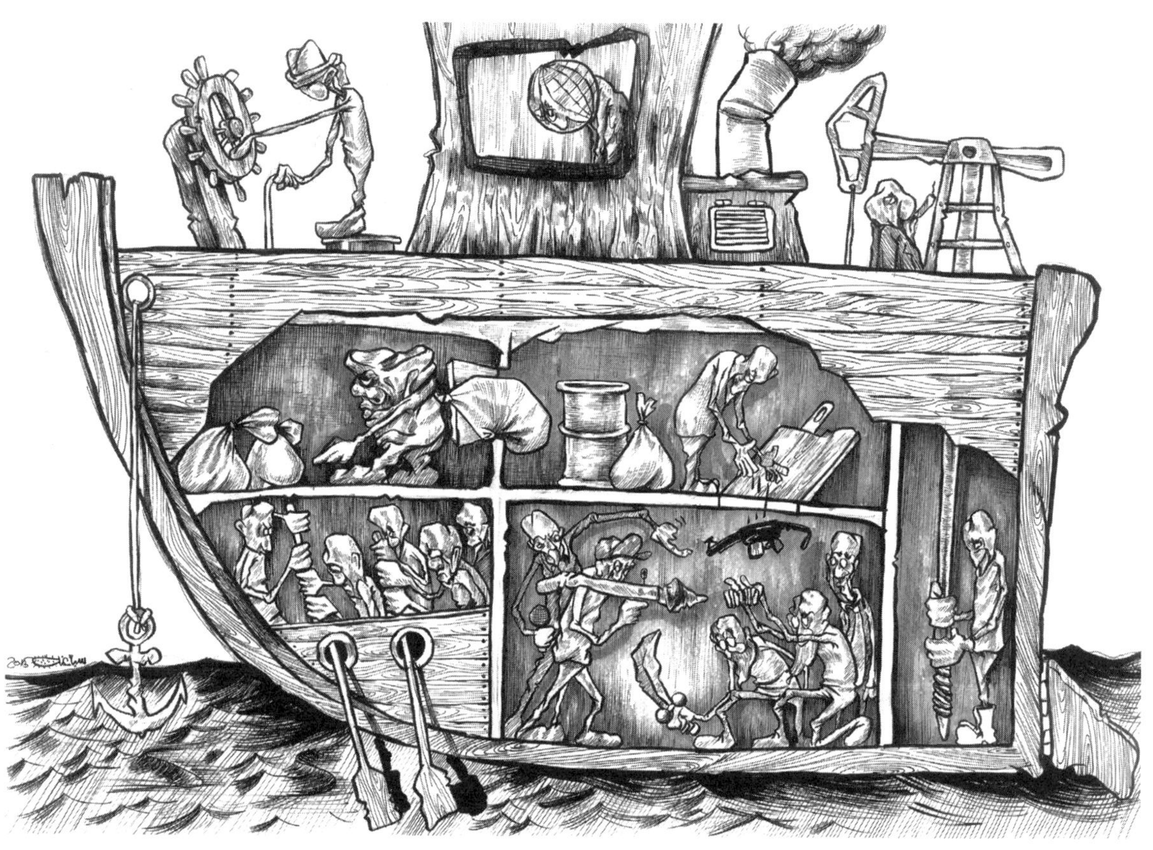

What takes place beneath the surface.

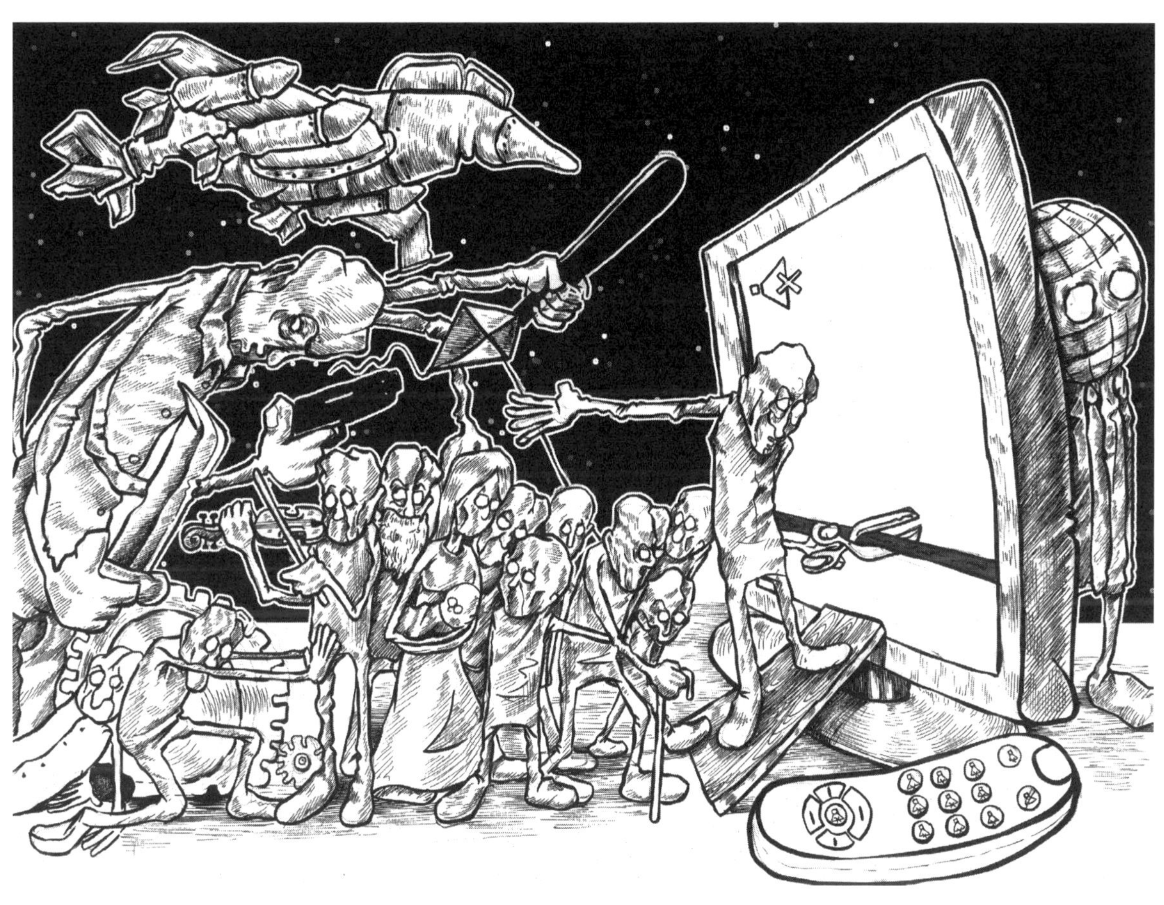

Breaking news (but keep it quiet).

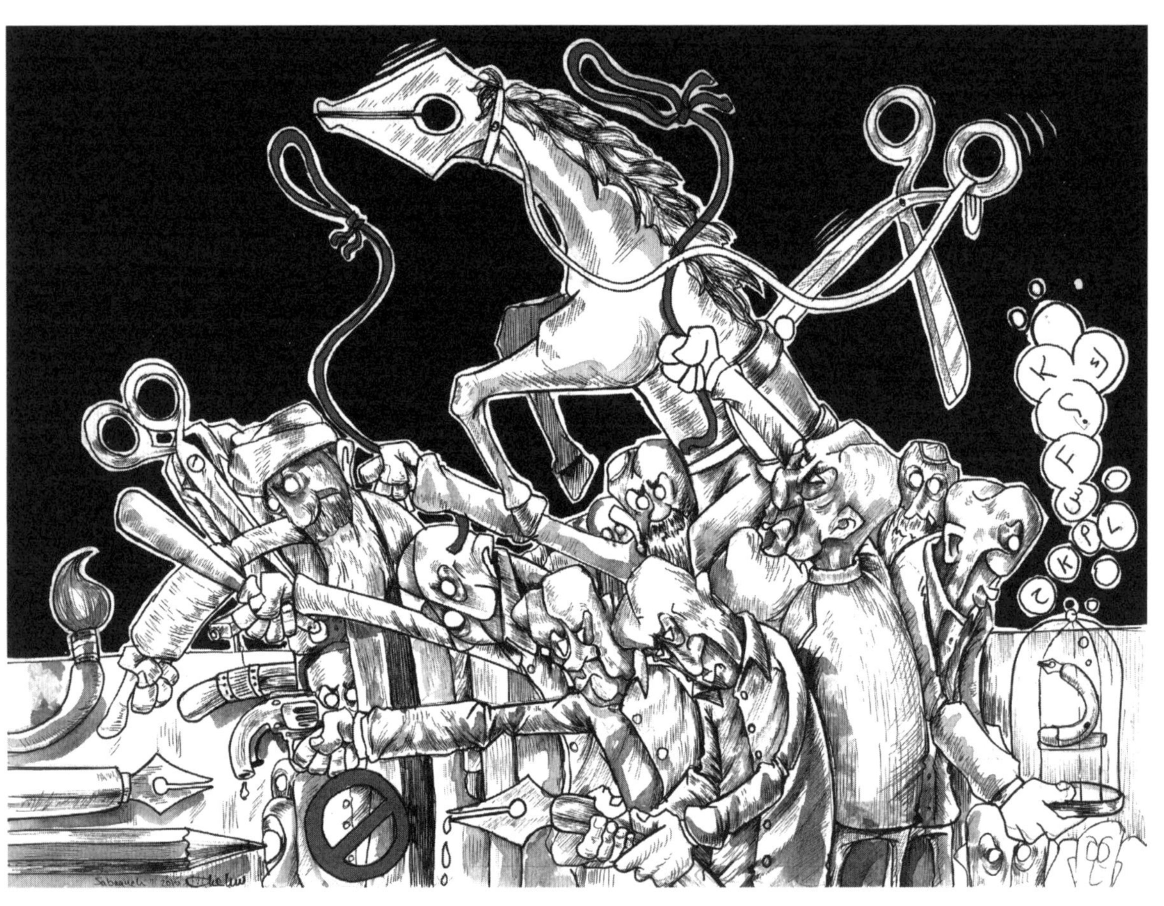

Freedom of expression as understood by religions and governments.

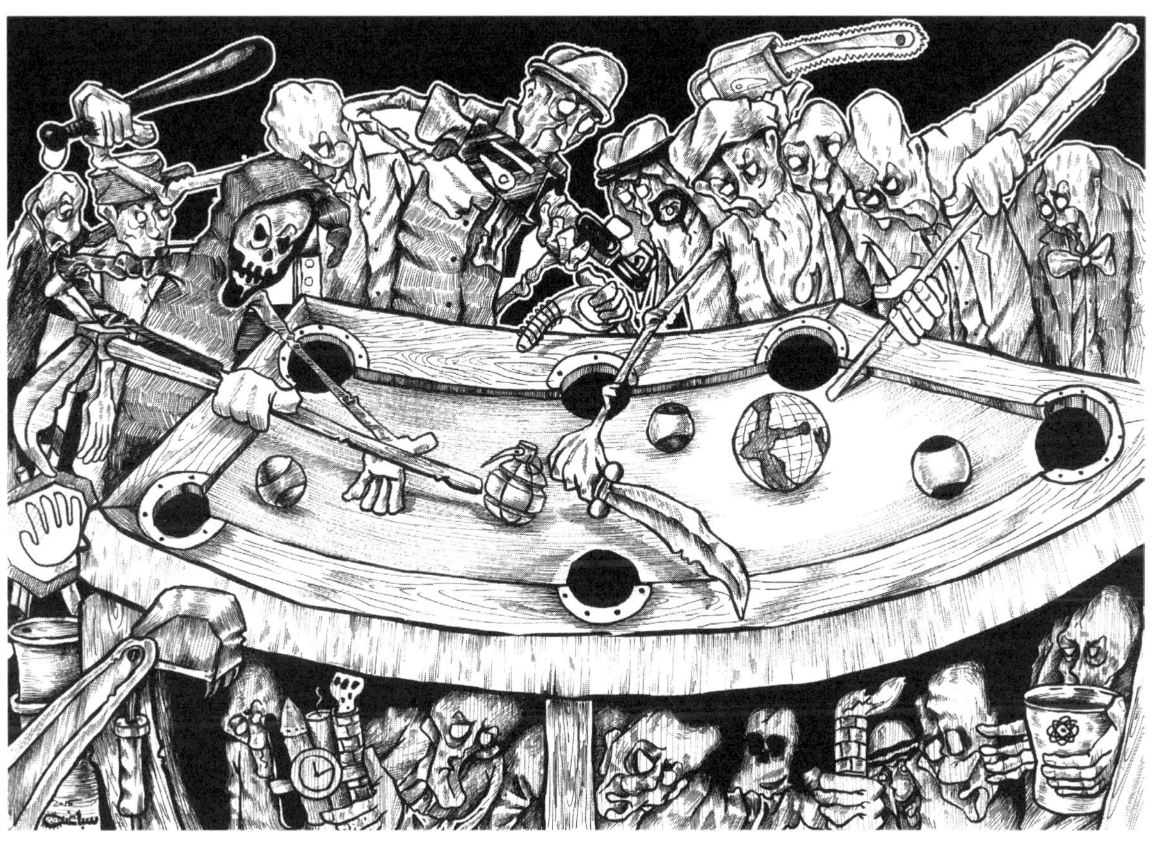

We fight for the same resources and pursue our individual interests.

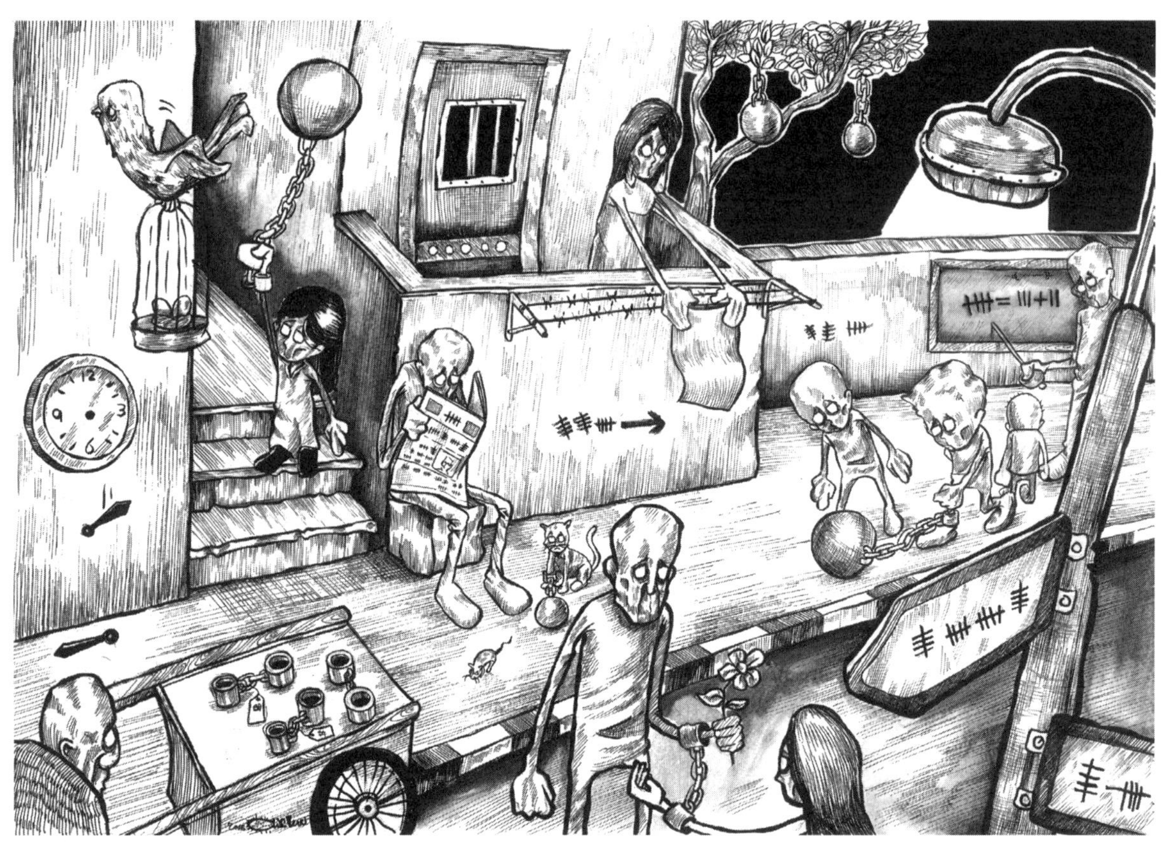

A kind of existence.

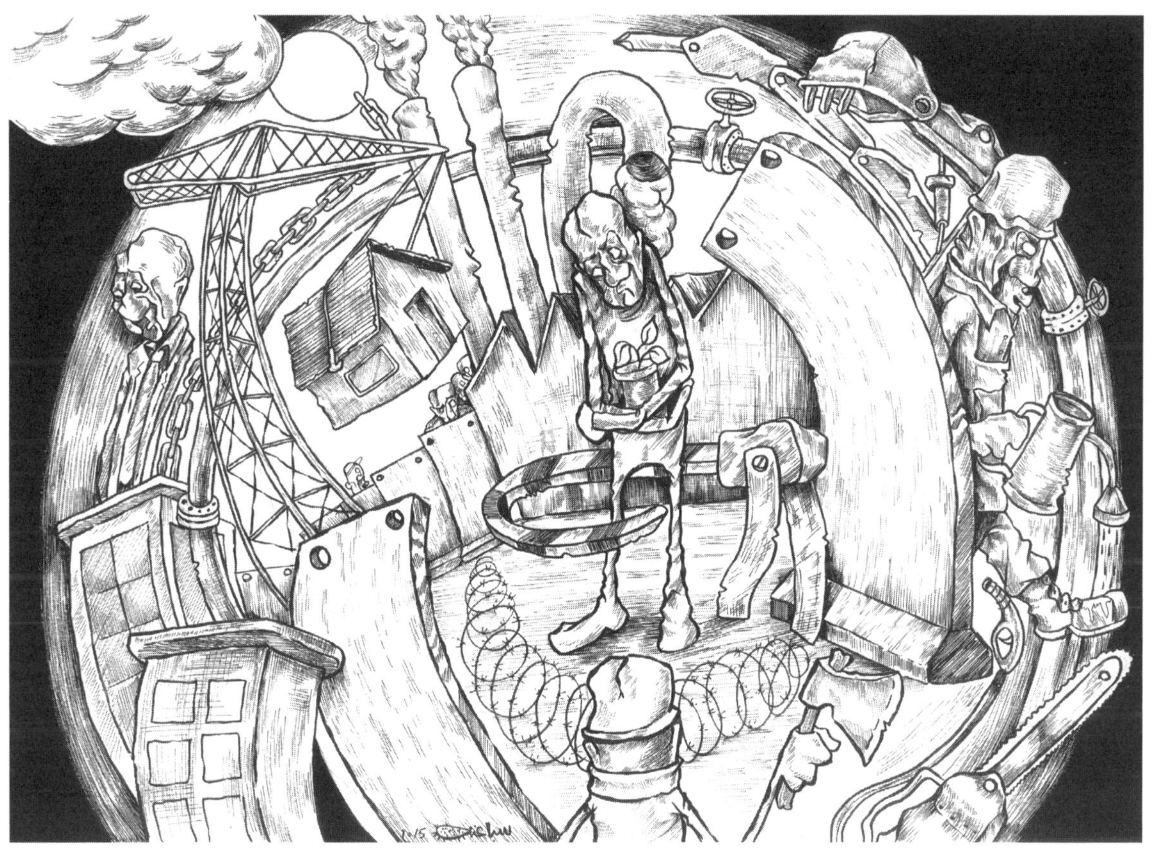

Trapped.

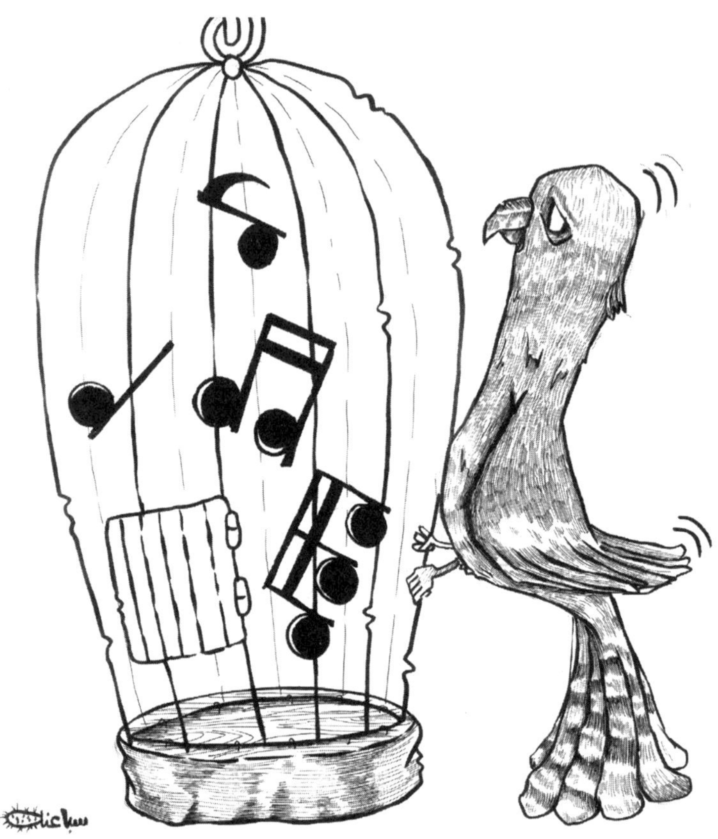

We sing freedom.

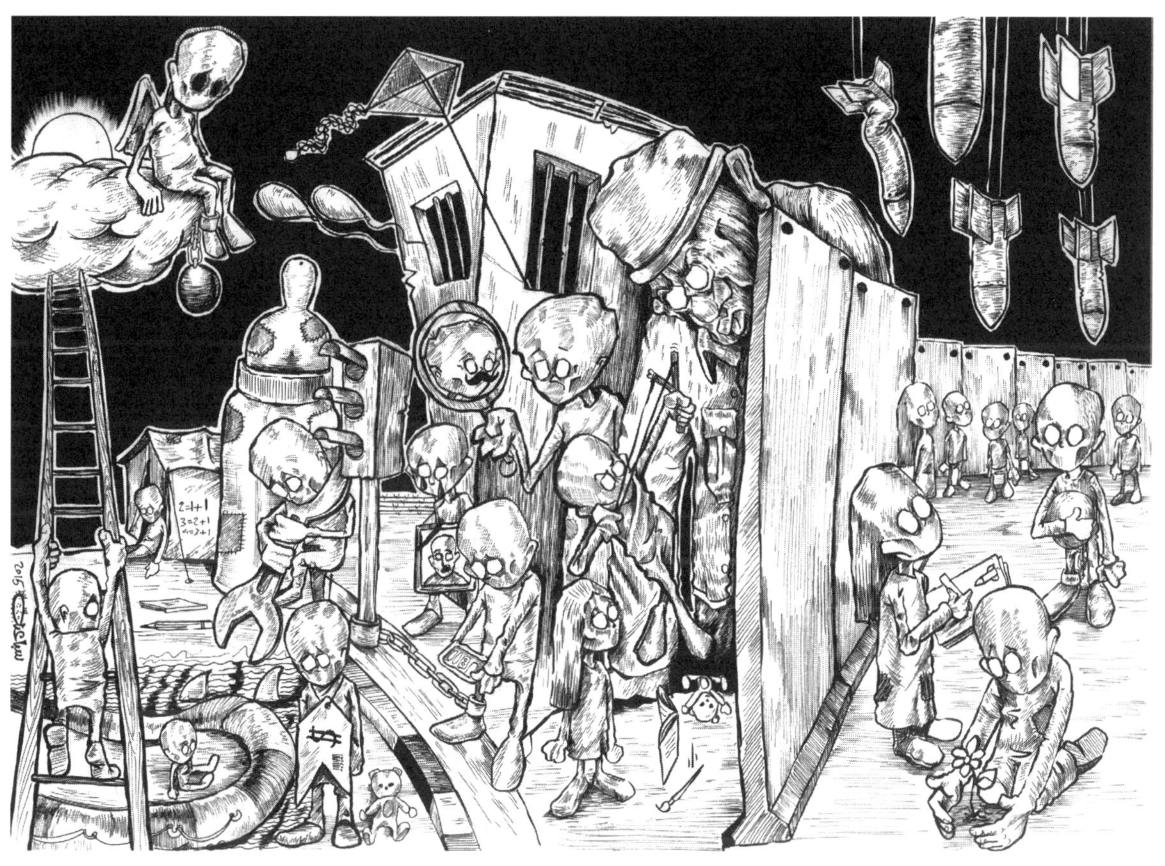
2=1+1
3=2+1
4=3+1

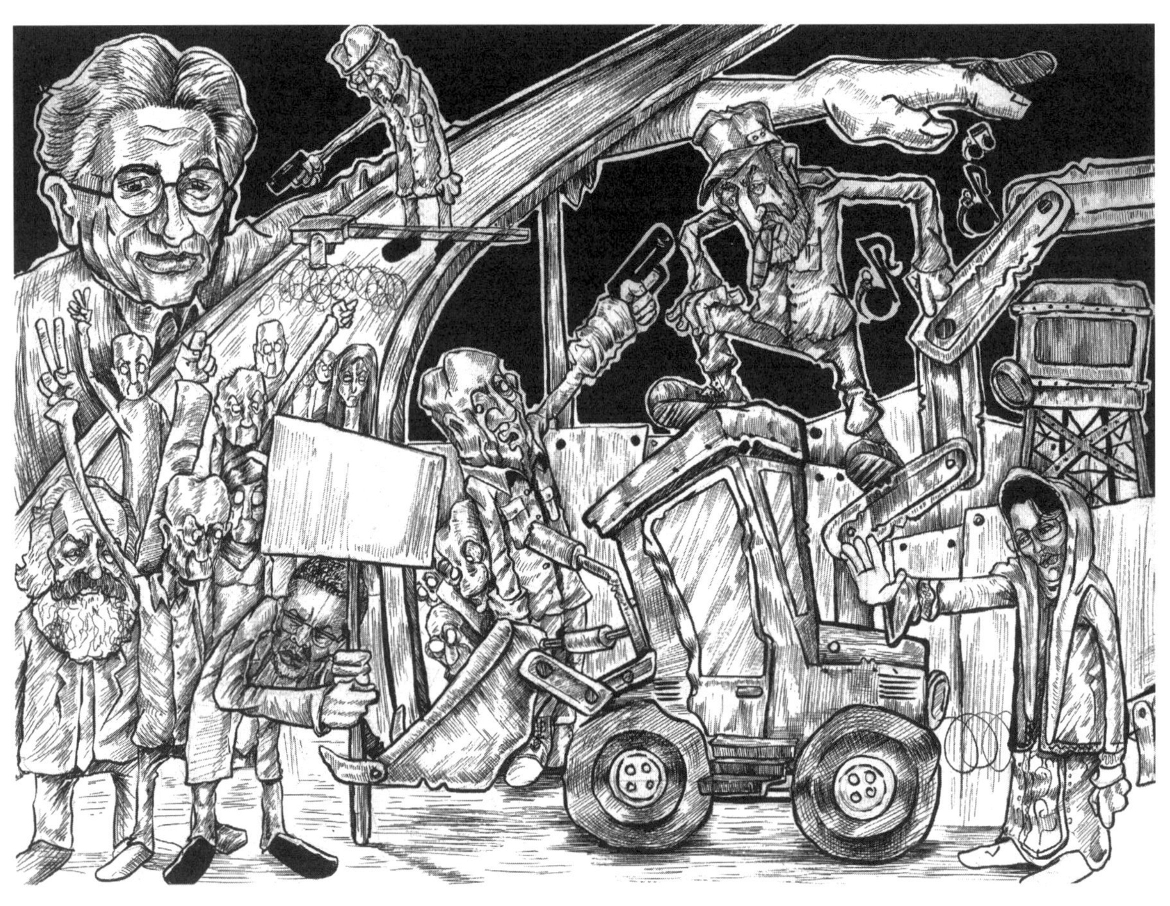

How will history judge the torment of Palestine?

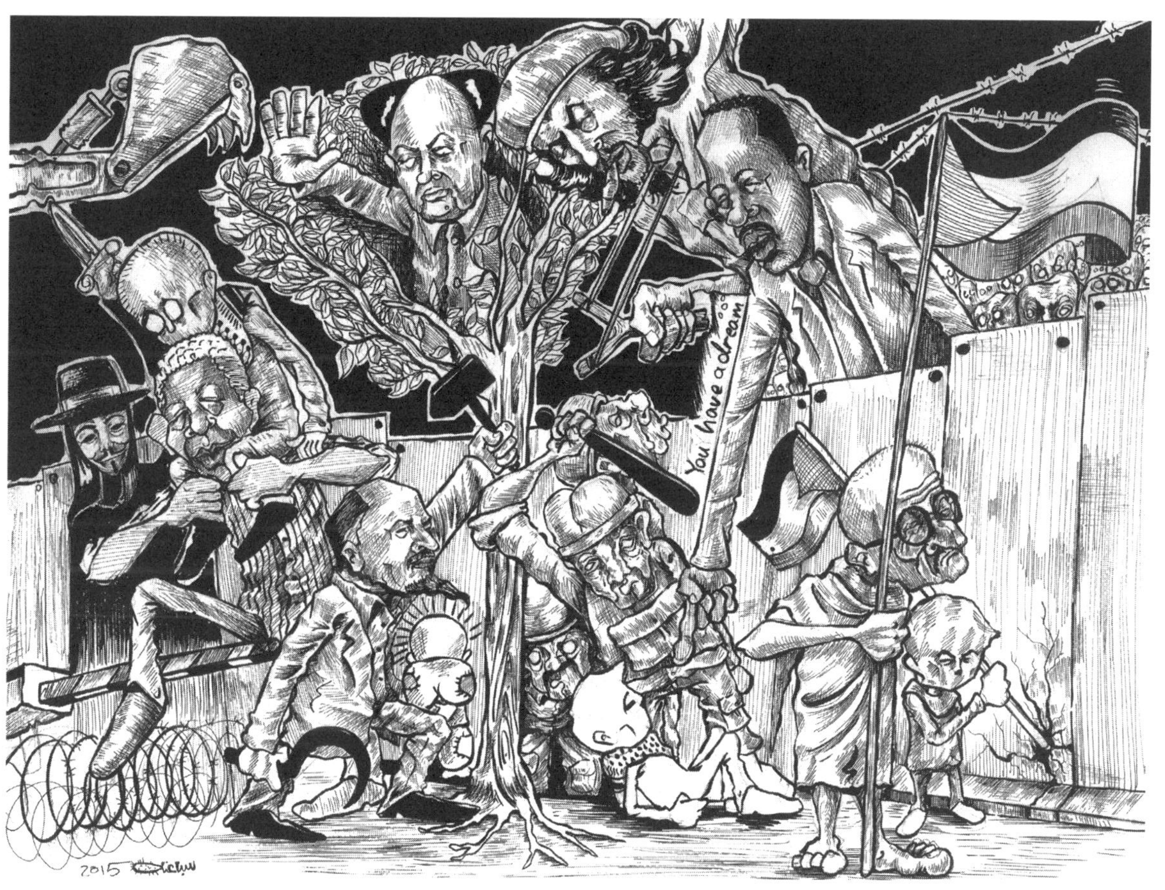

You have a dream
2015

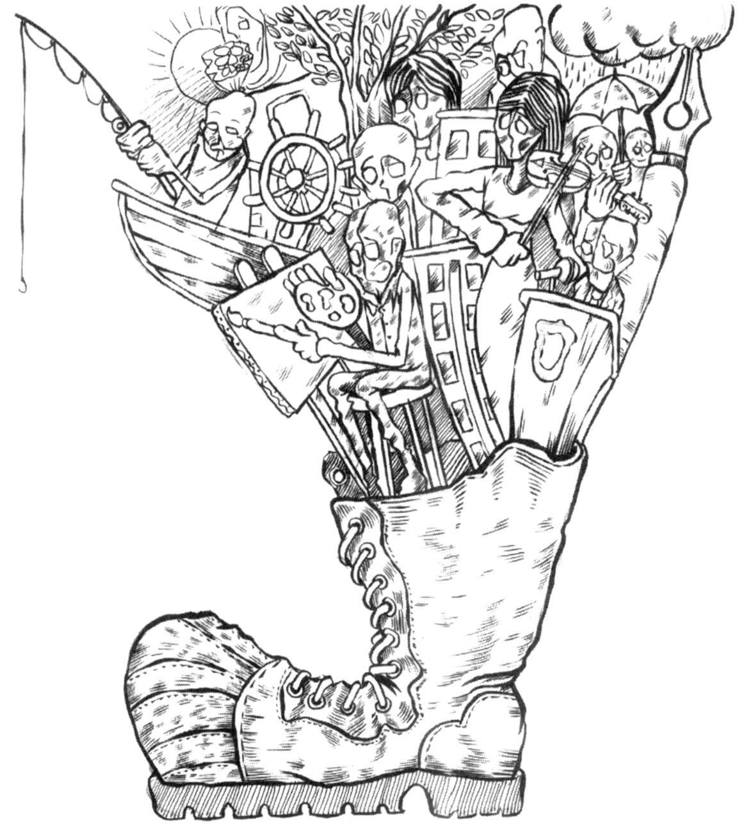

The army passed this way.

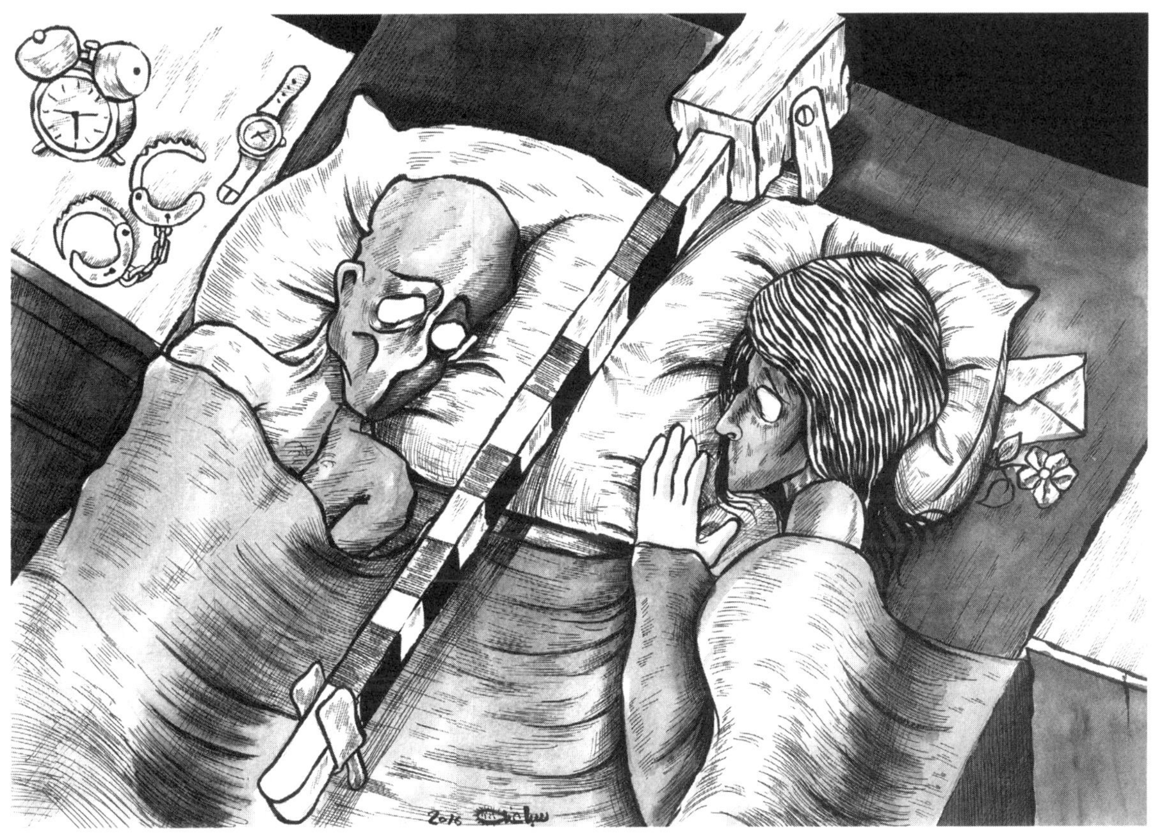

Someday we'll meet.

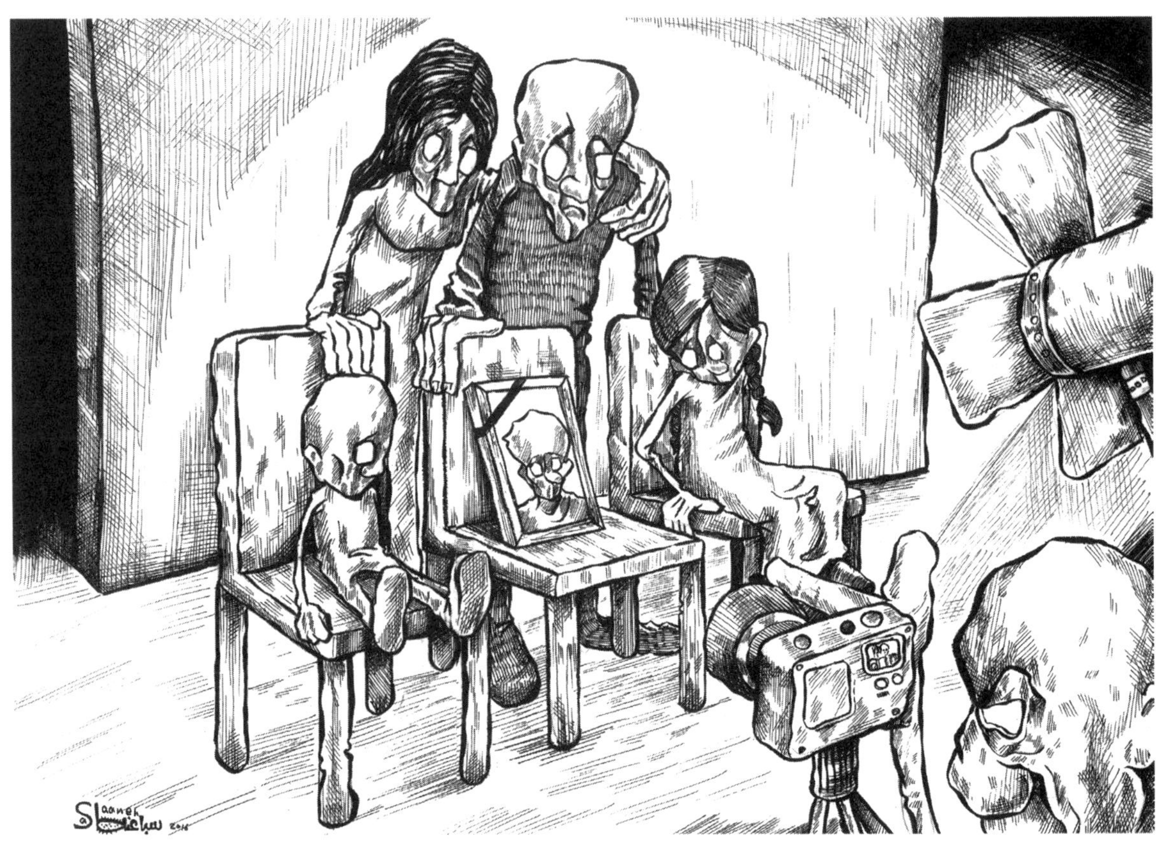

Family portrait.

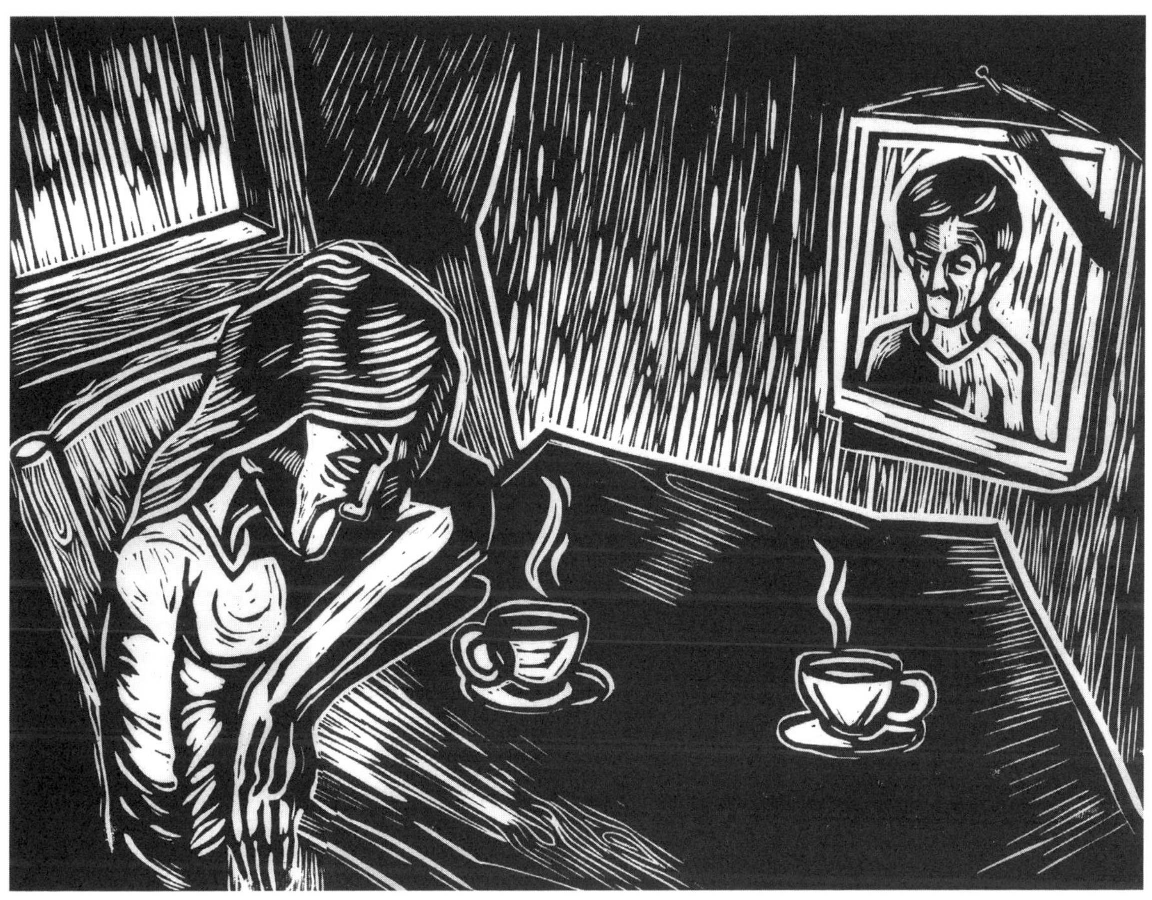

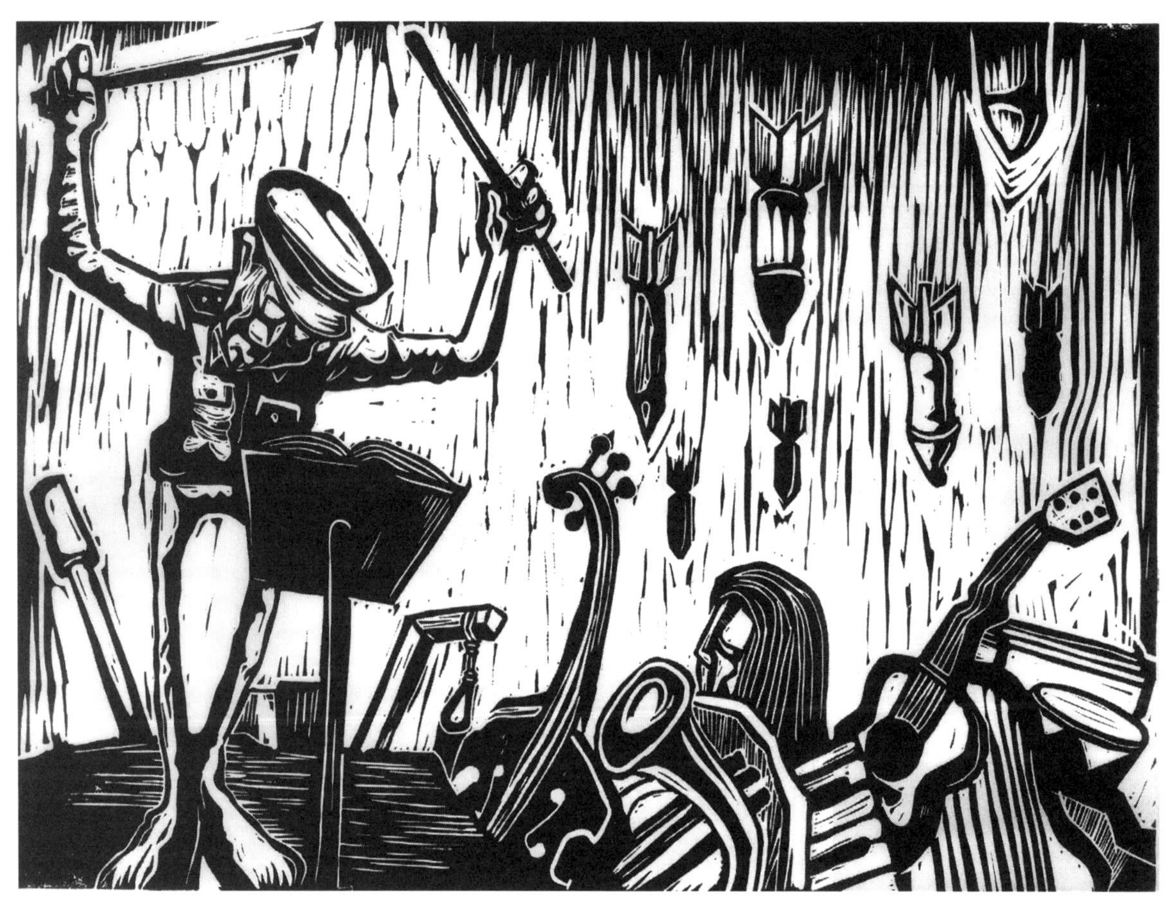

The dictator's melody.

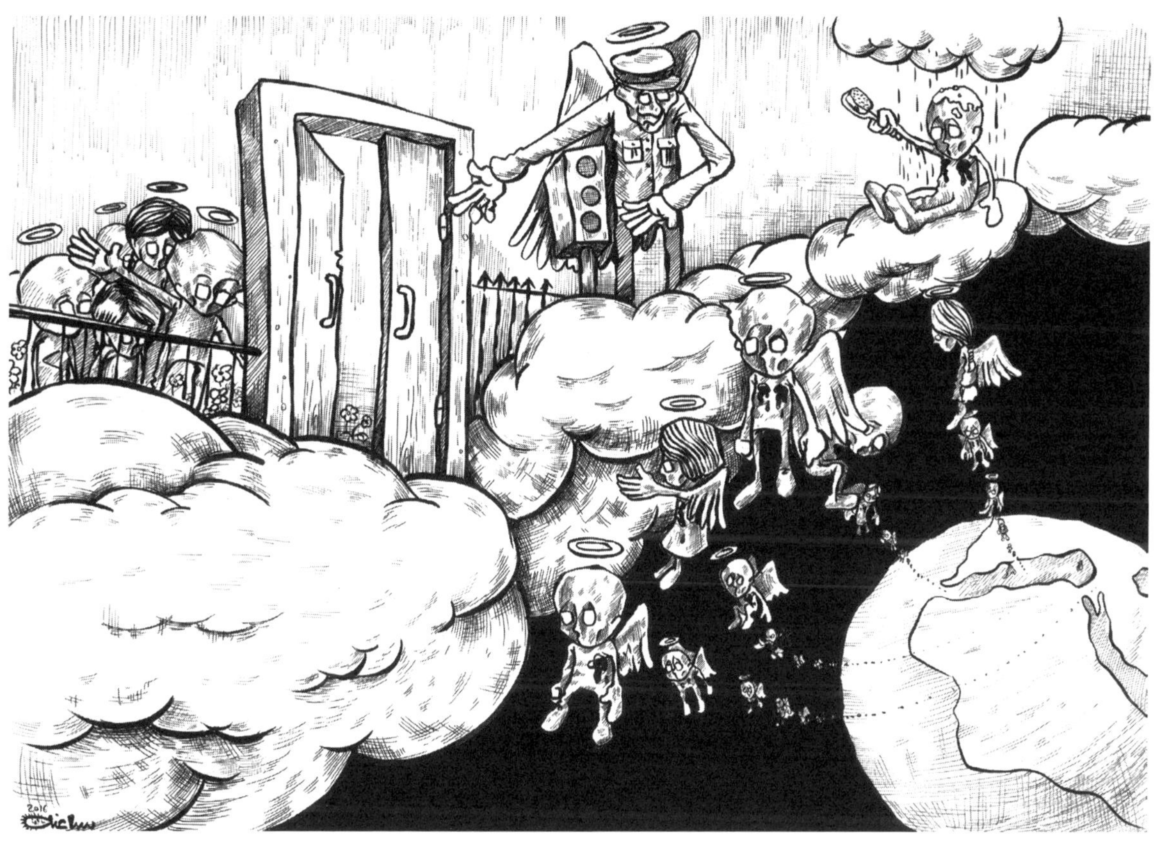

Child overcrowding.

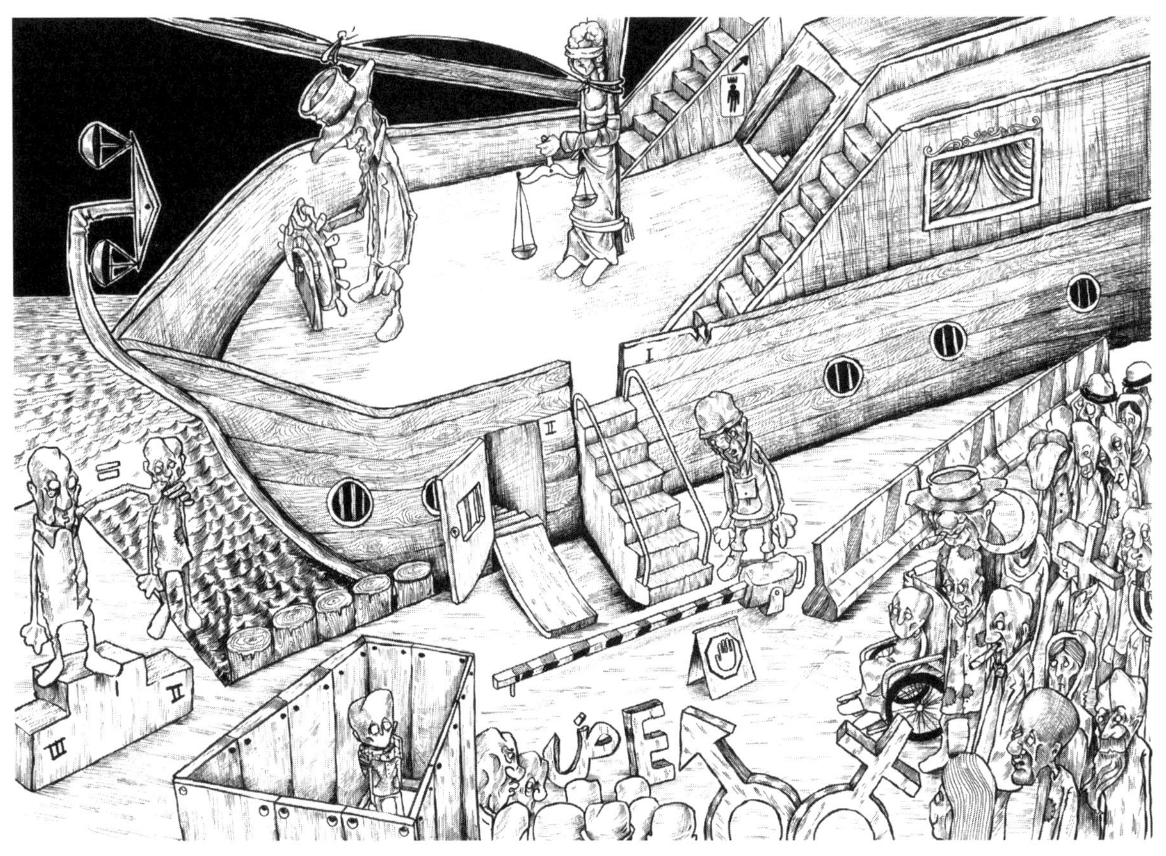

Who makes it onto the boat?

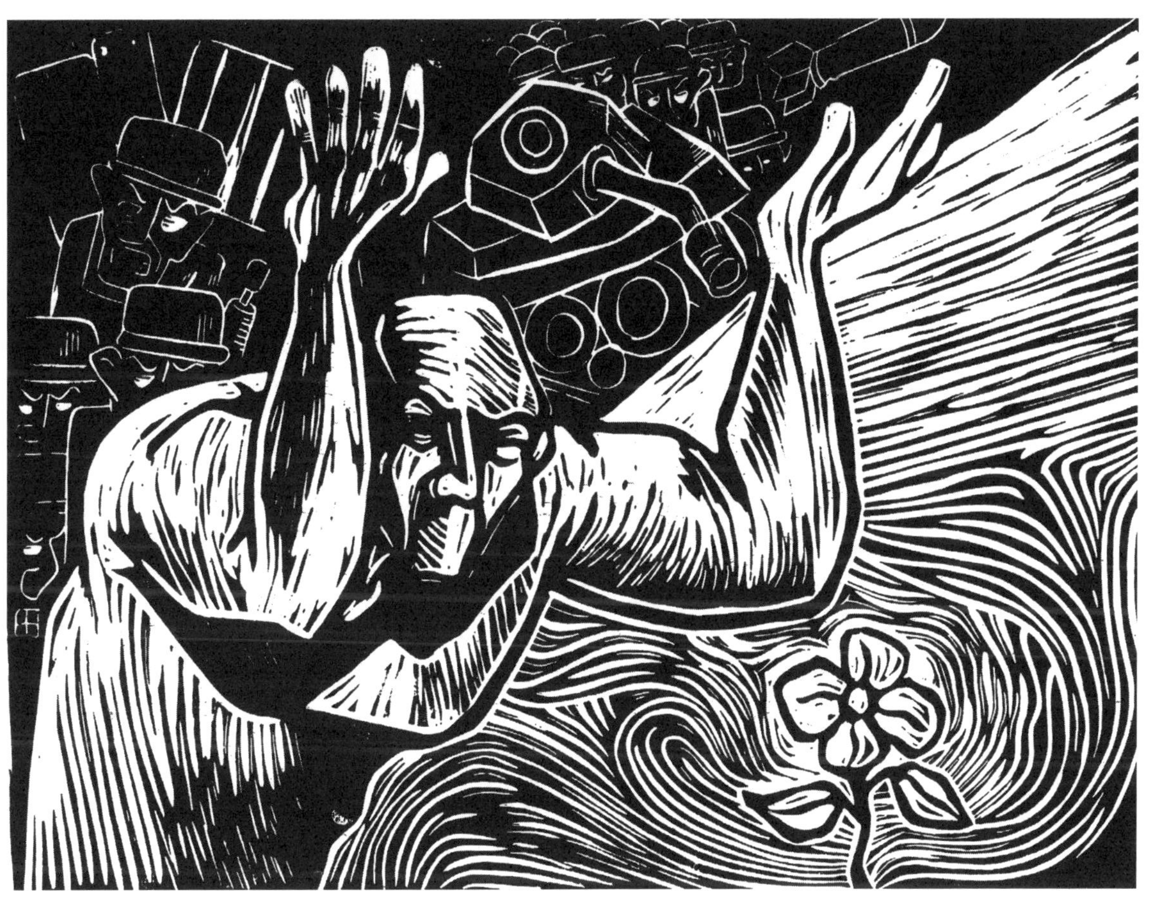

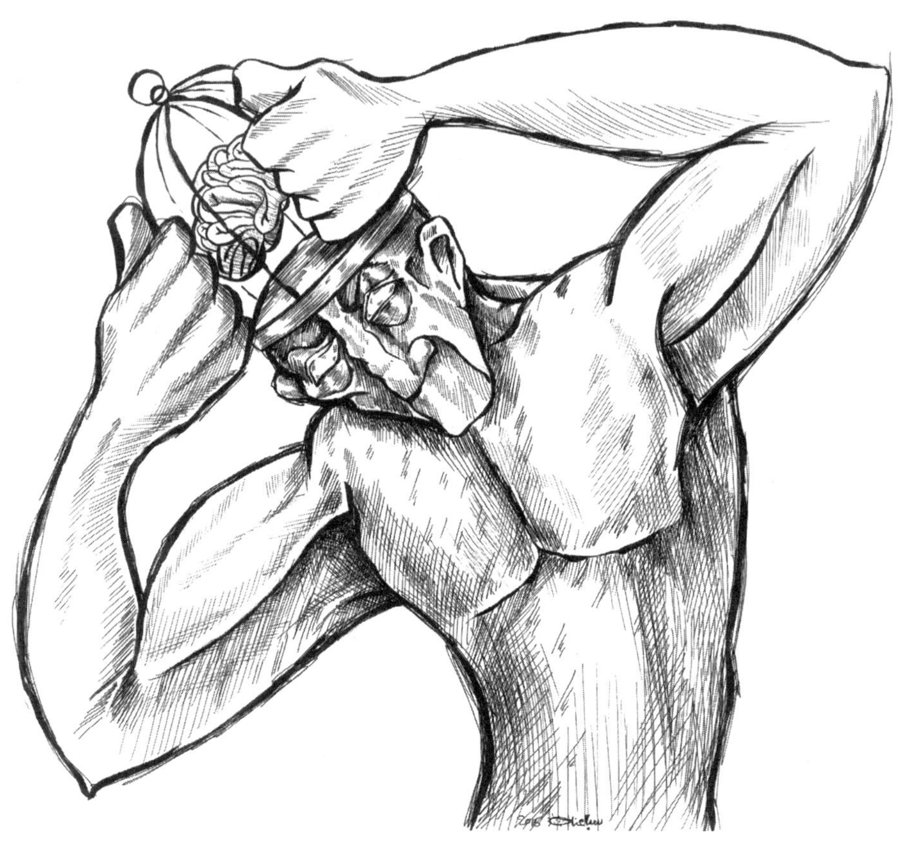

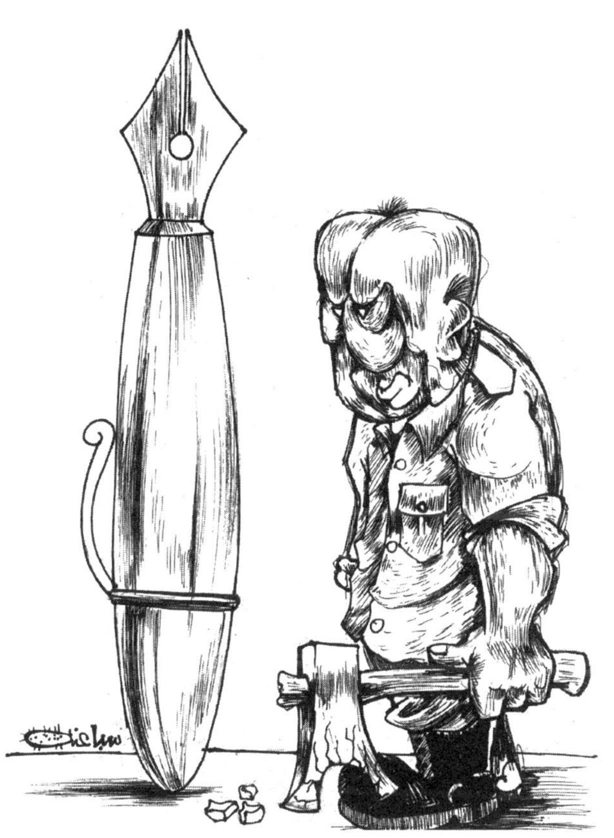
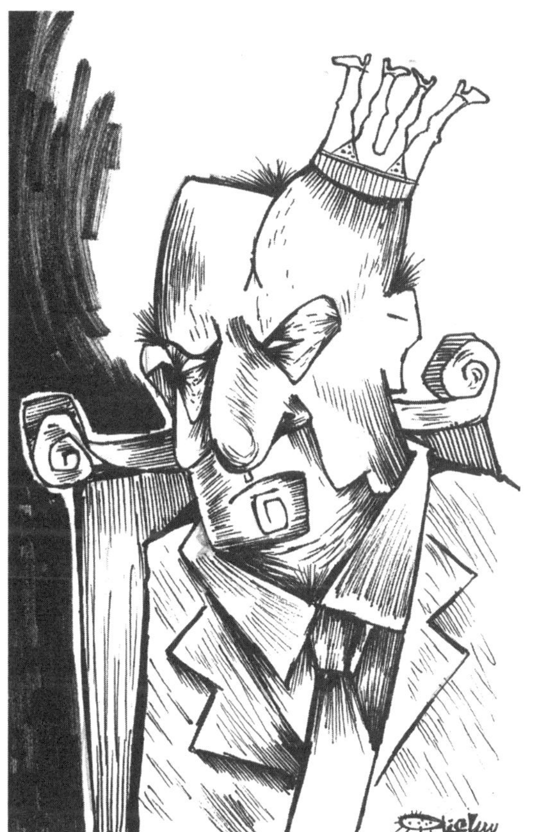

Dictator.

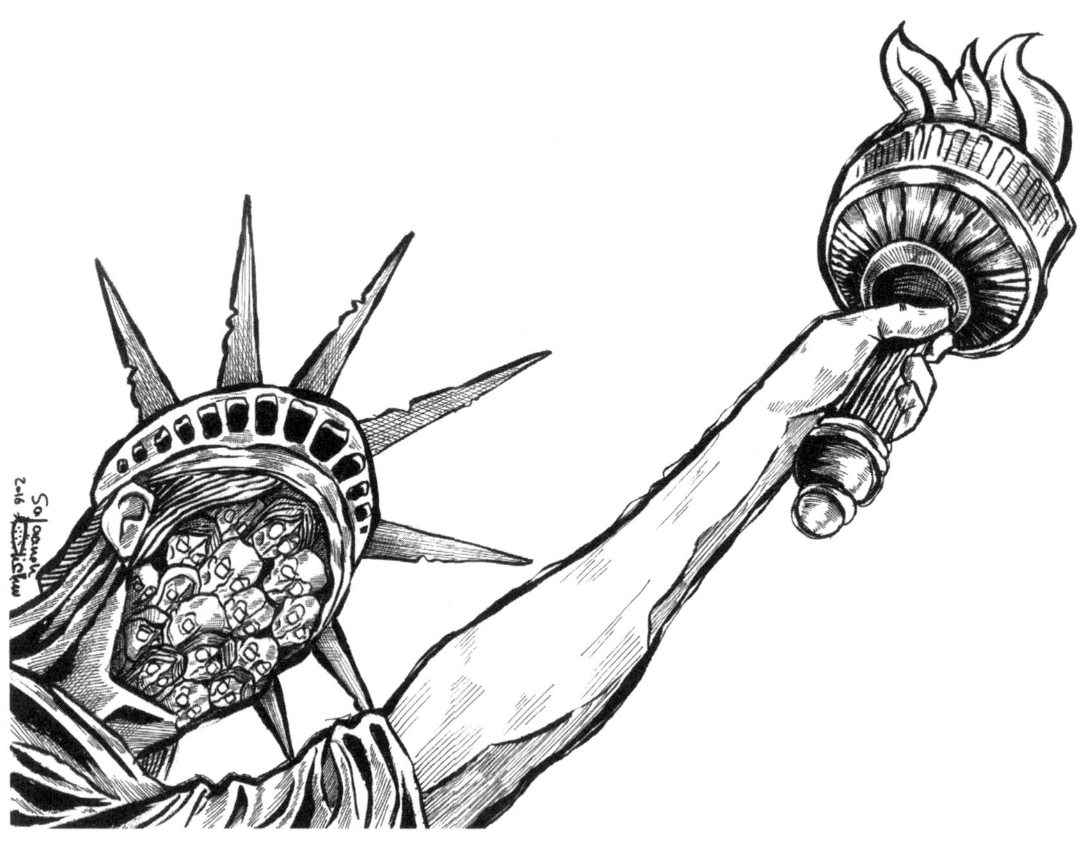

Nations are the symbols of freedom.

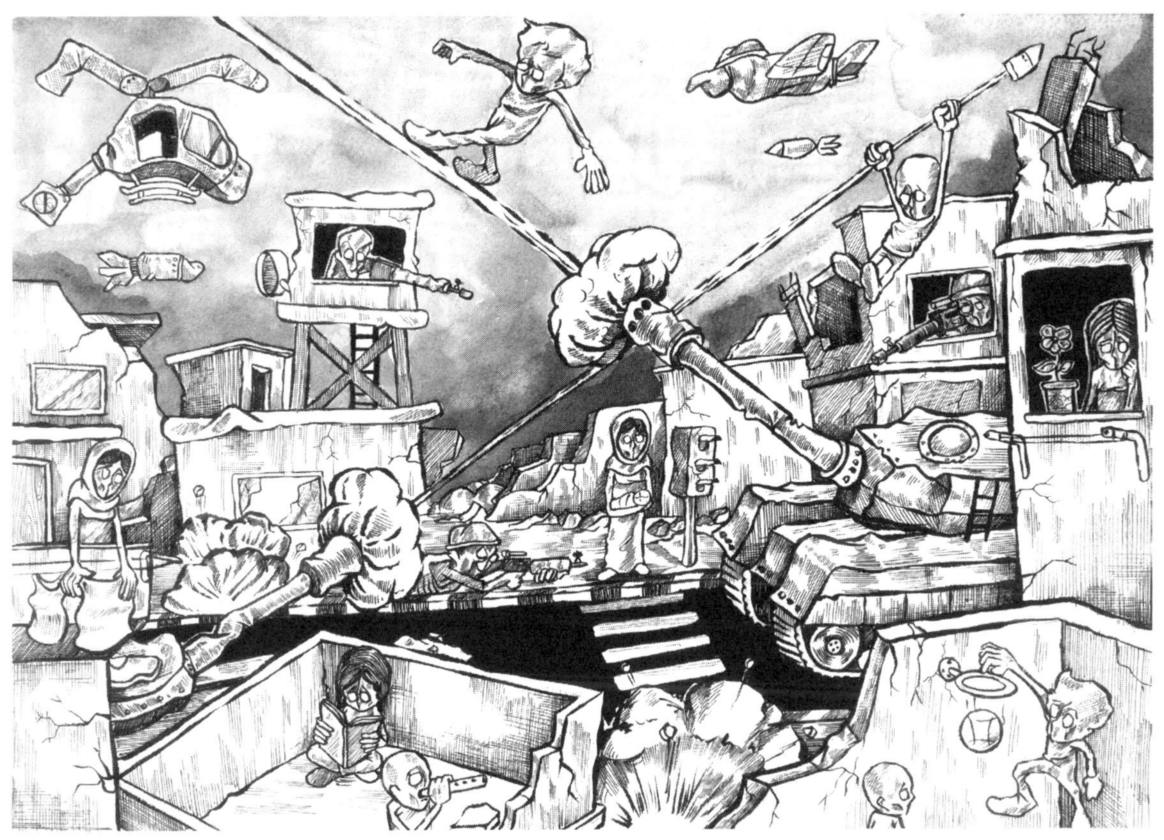

We need space to live amid the crush of death.

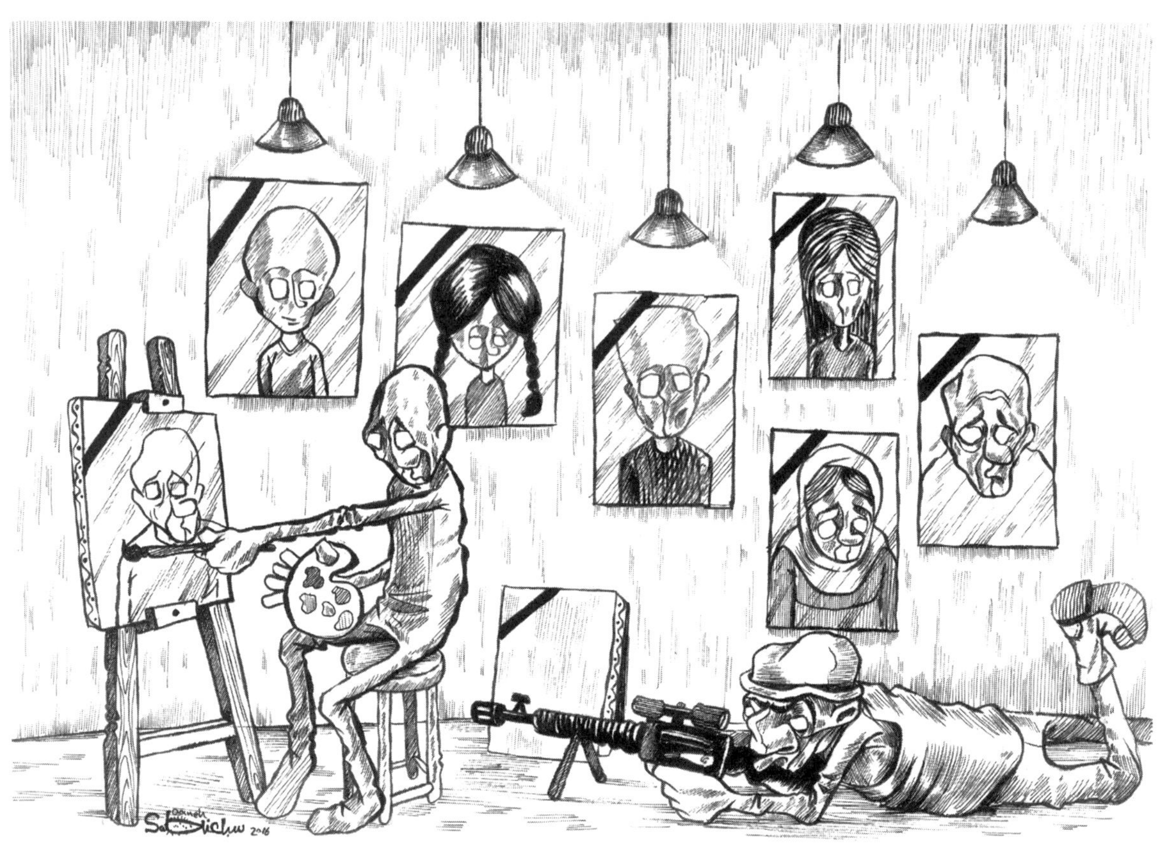

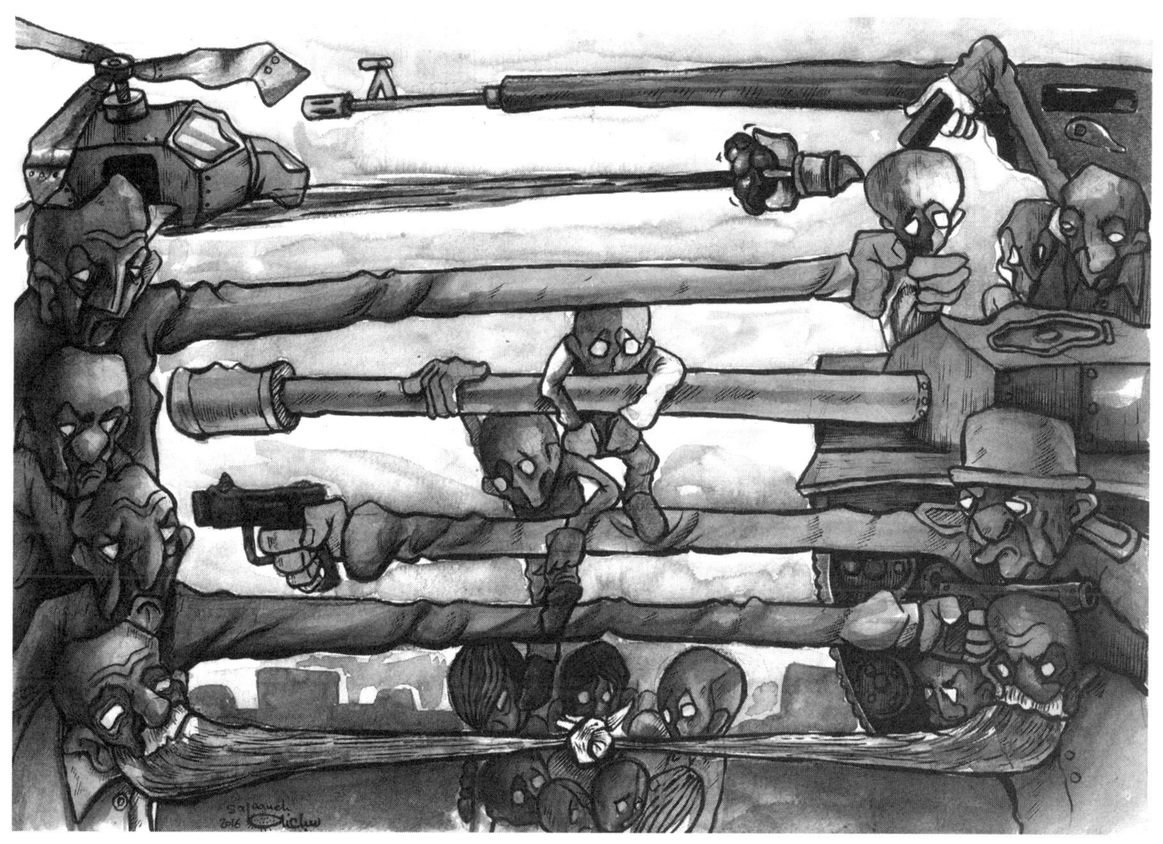

War is never-ending.

4

POLITICAL PRISONERS

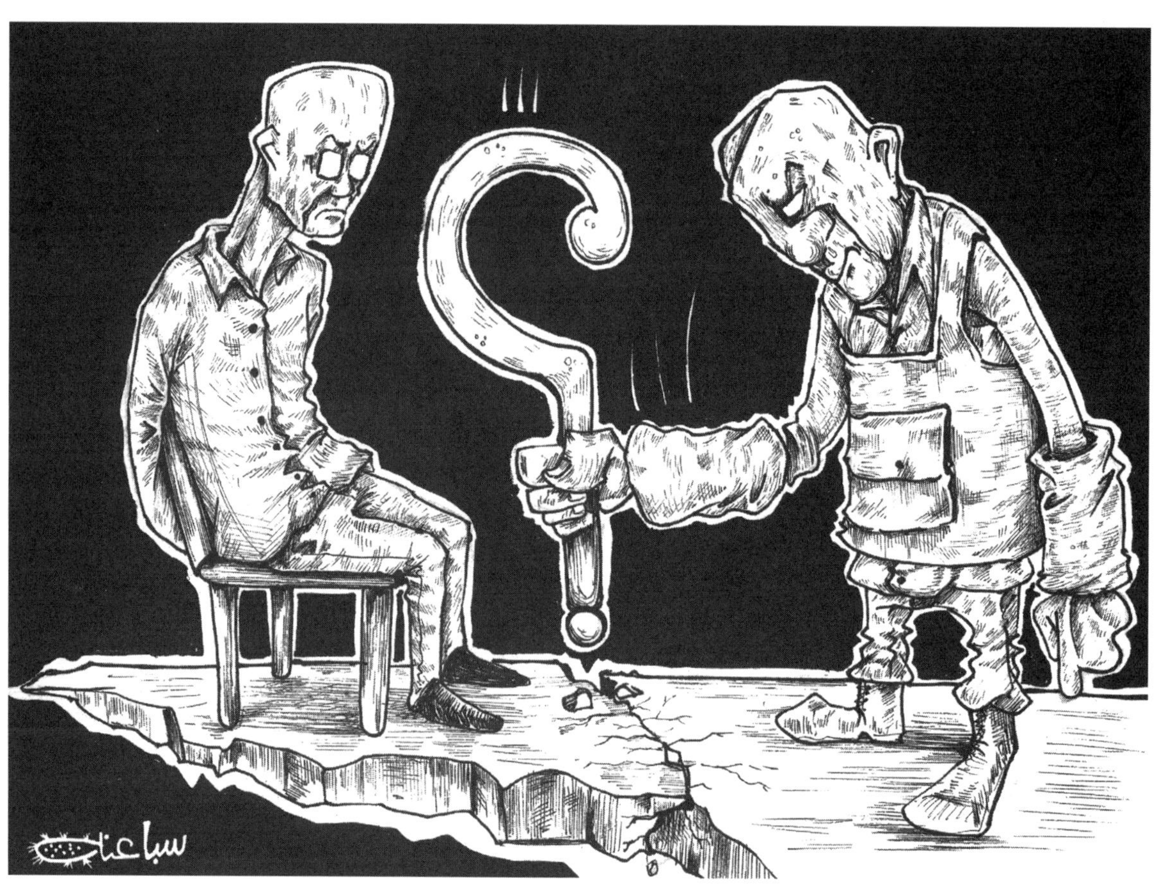

The prisoner's only weapon during interrogation is patience.

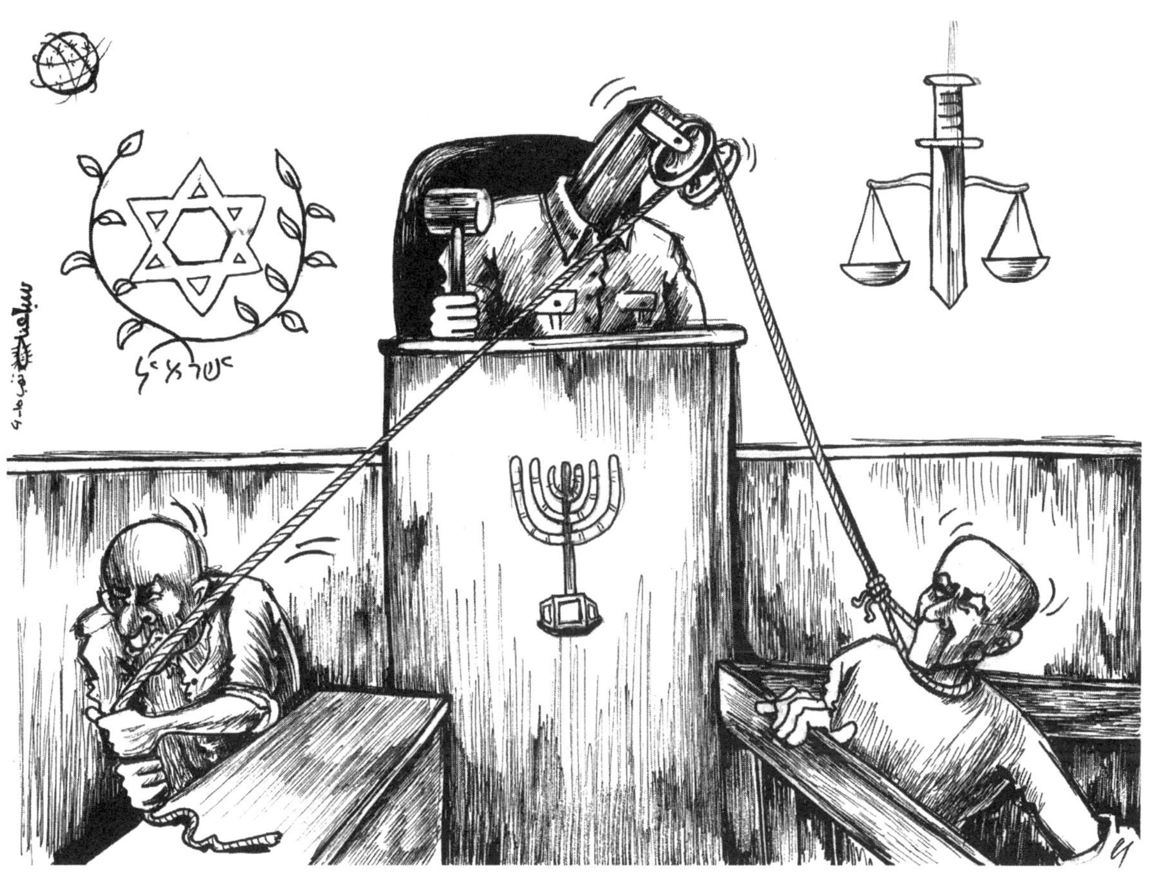

The judiciary is just another tool in the hands of the jailer.

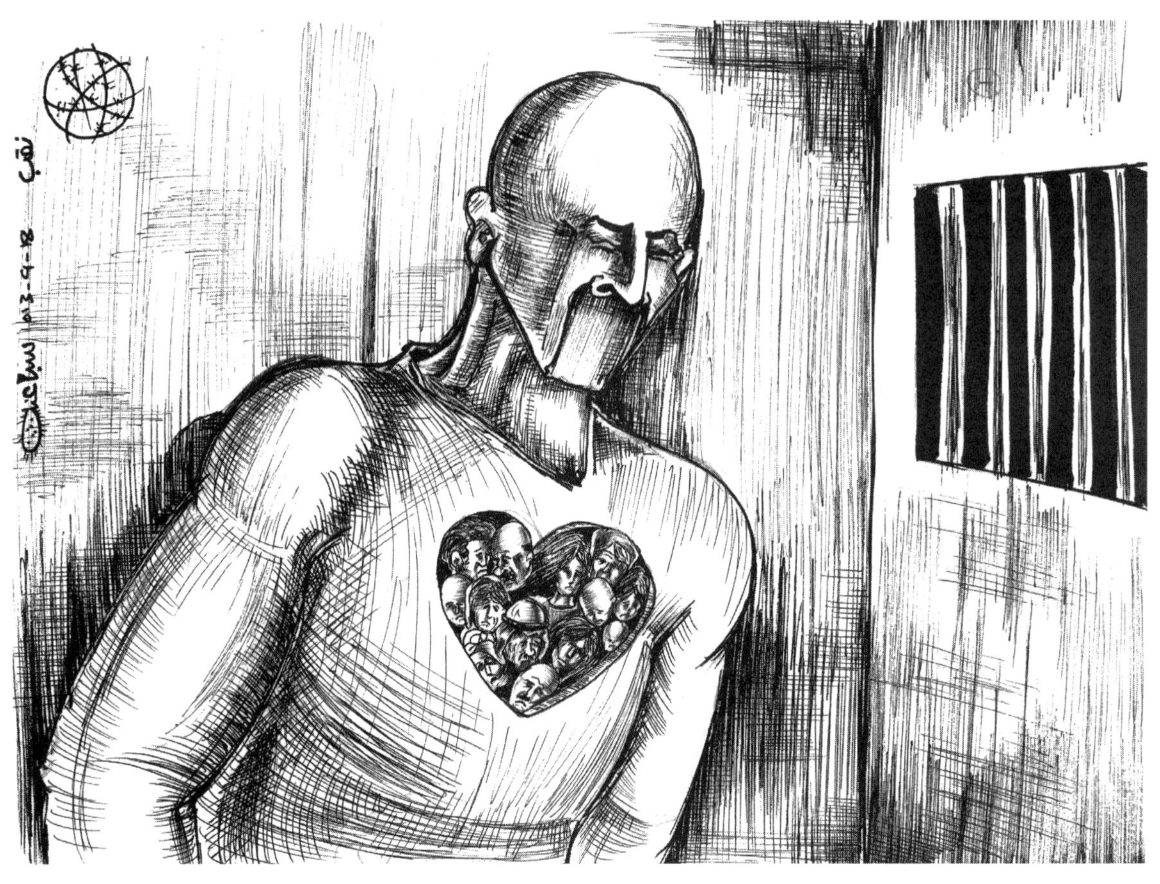

My homeland lives in my heart.

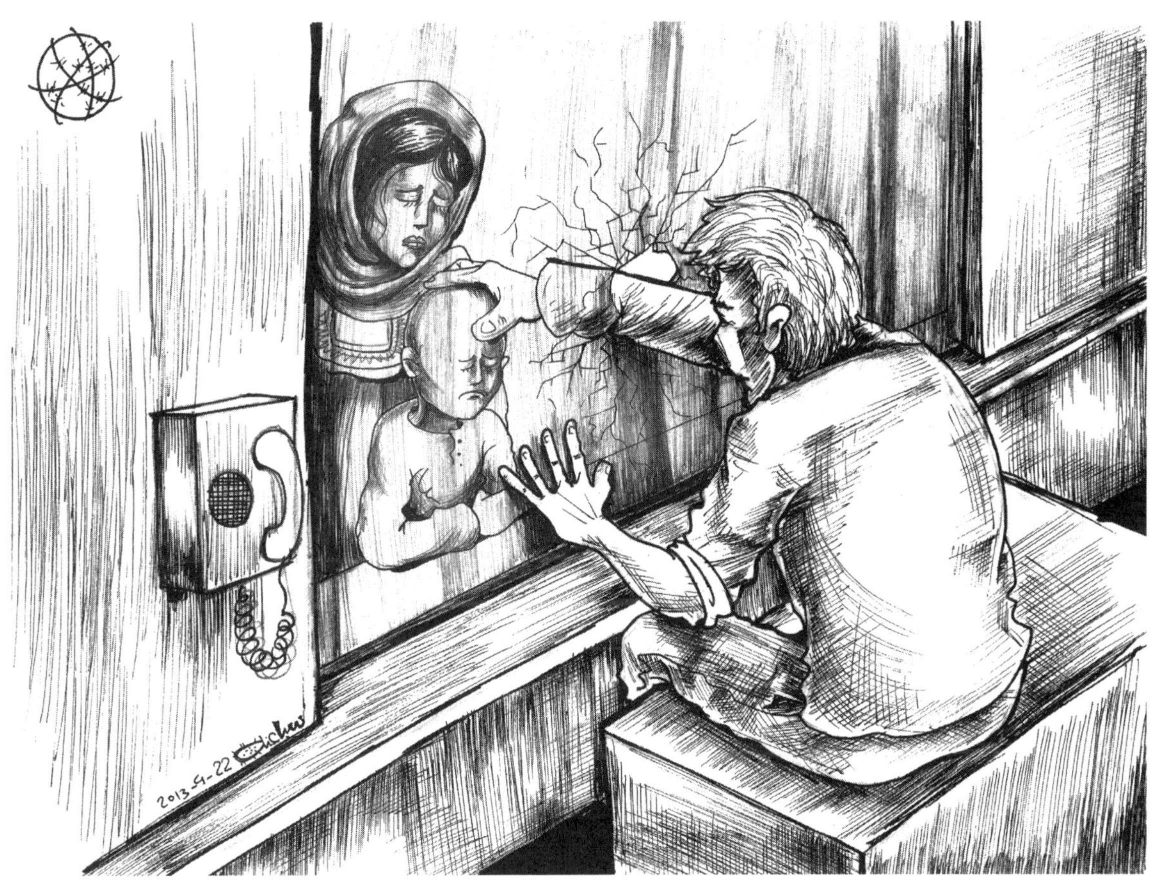

2013-9-22

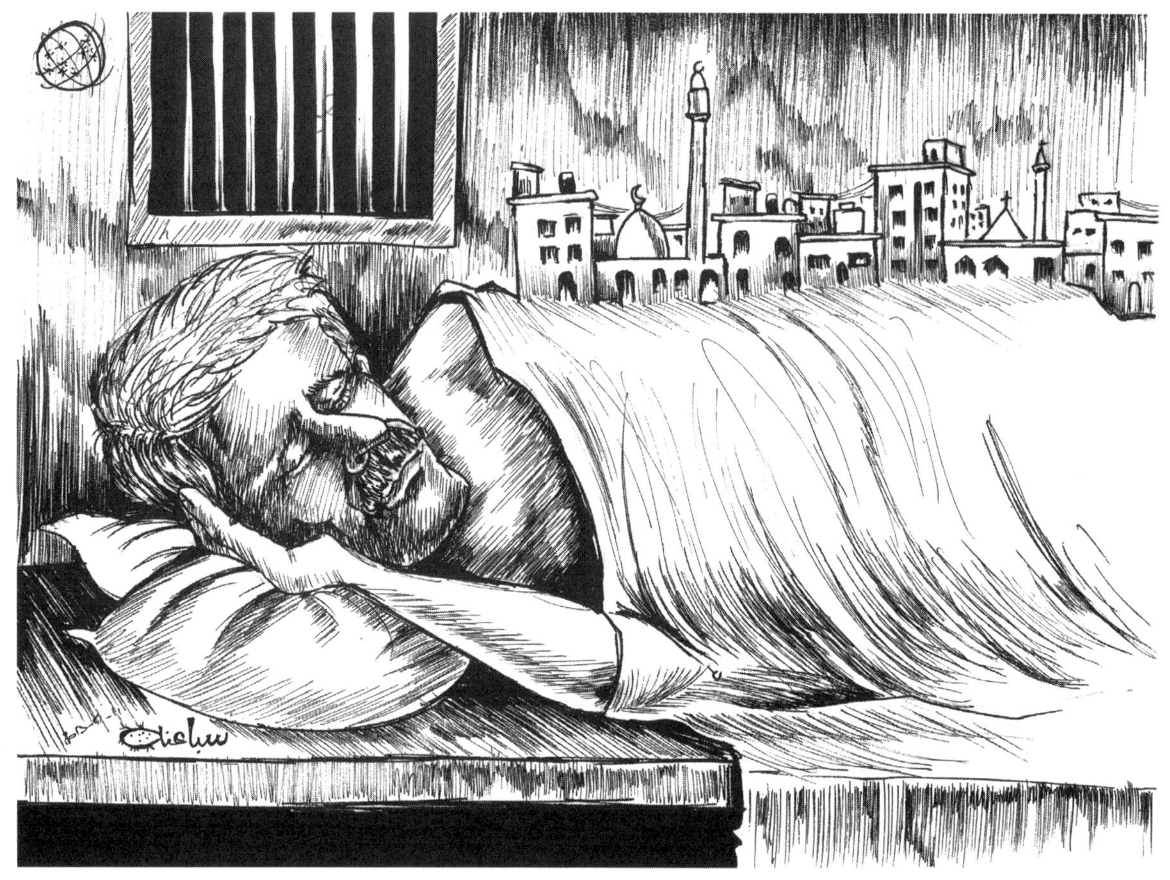

Dreaming of home.

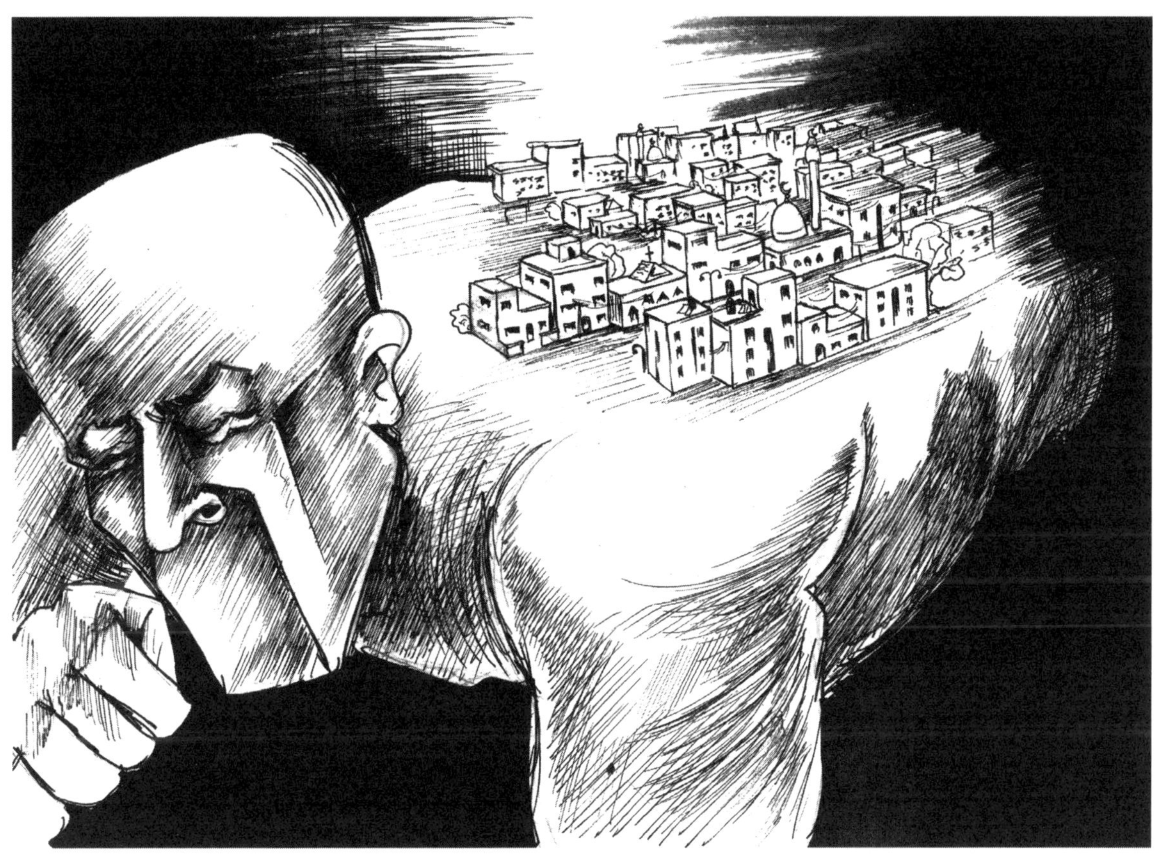

Prisoners carry the weight of their homeland.

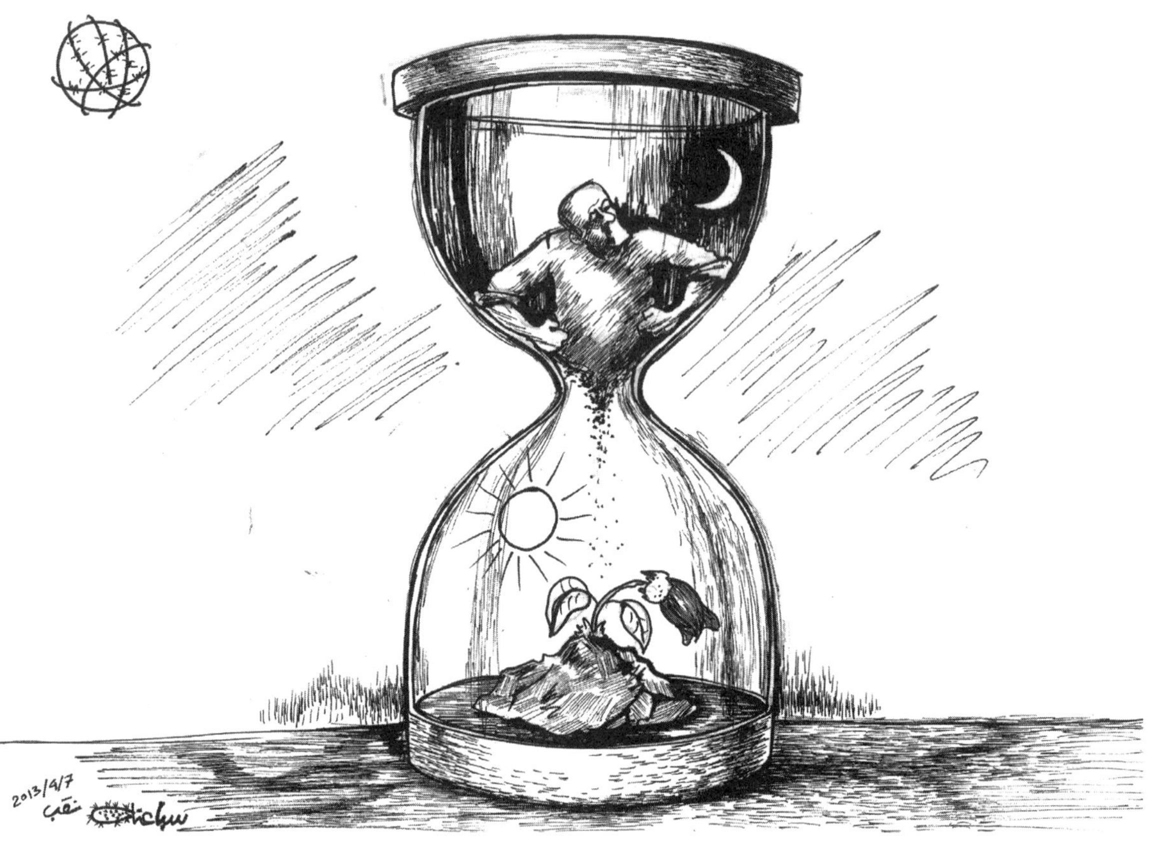

They pay with the best years of their lives.

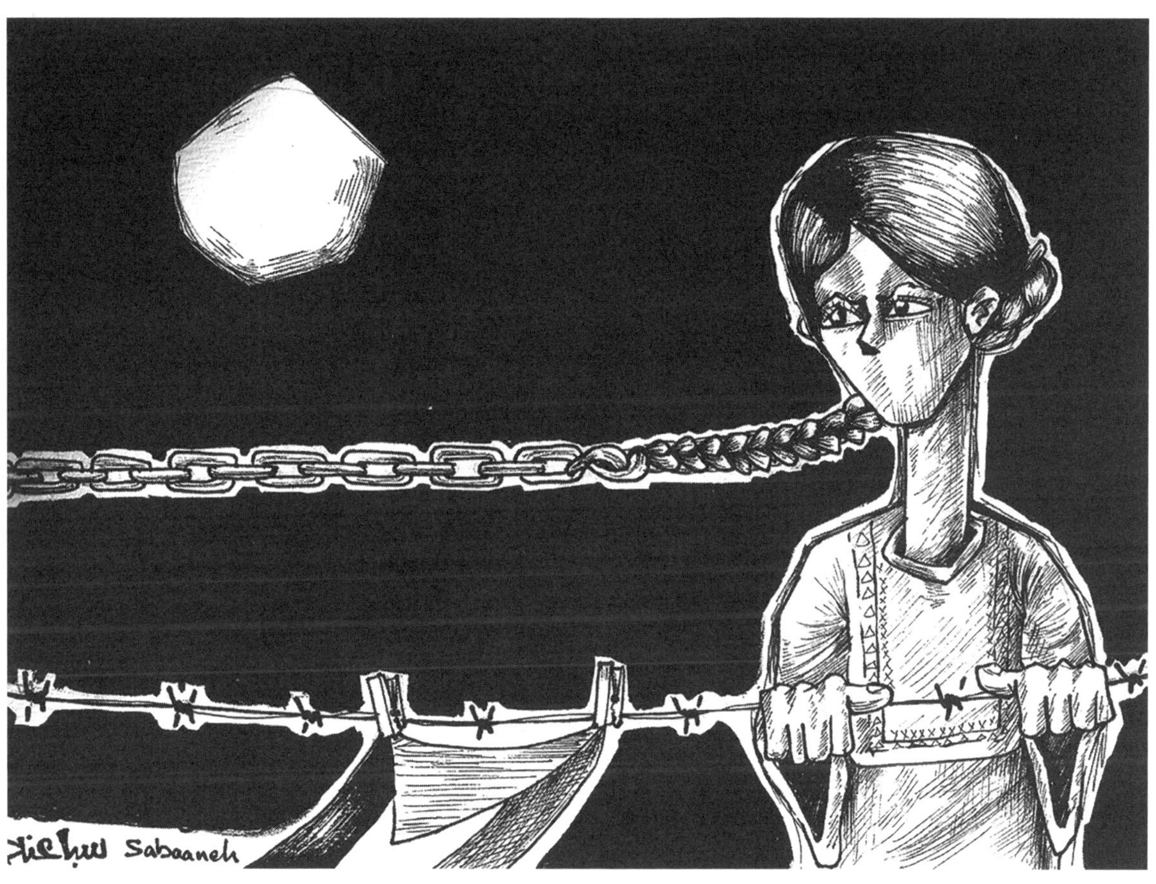

Women prisoners.

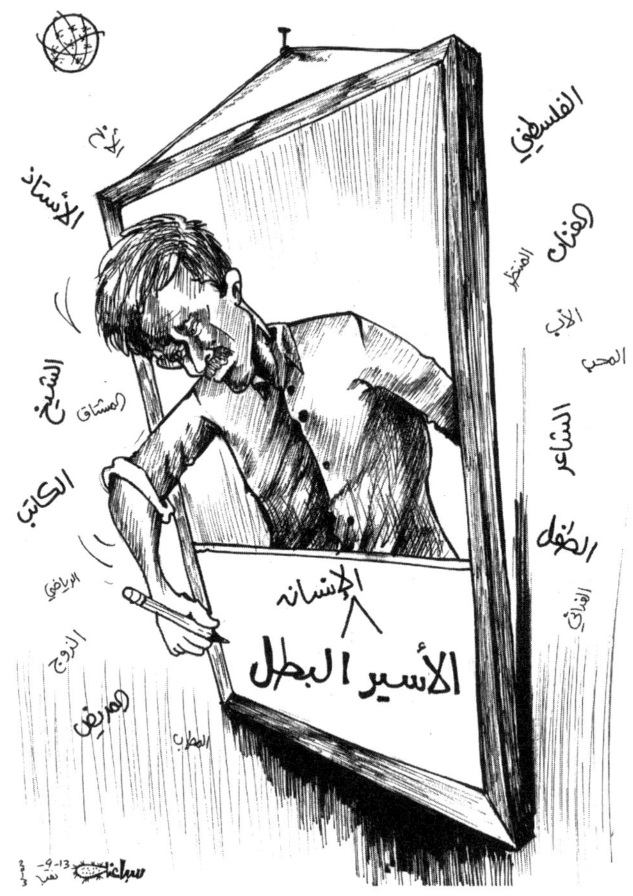

The "hero-prisoner" is a father, brother, poet, teacher – and a human being.

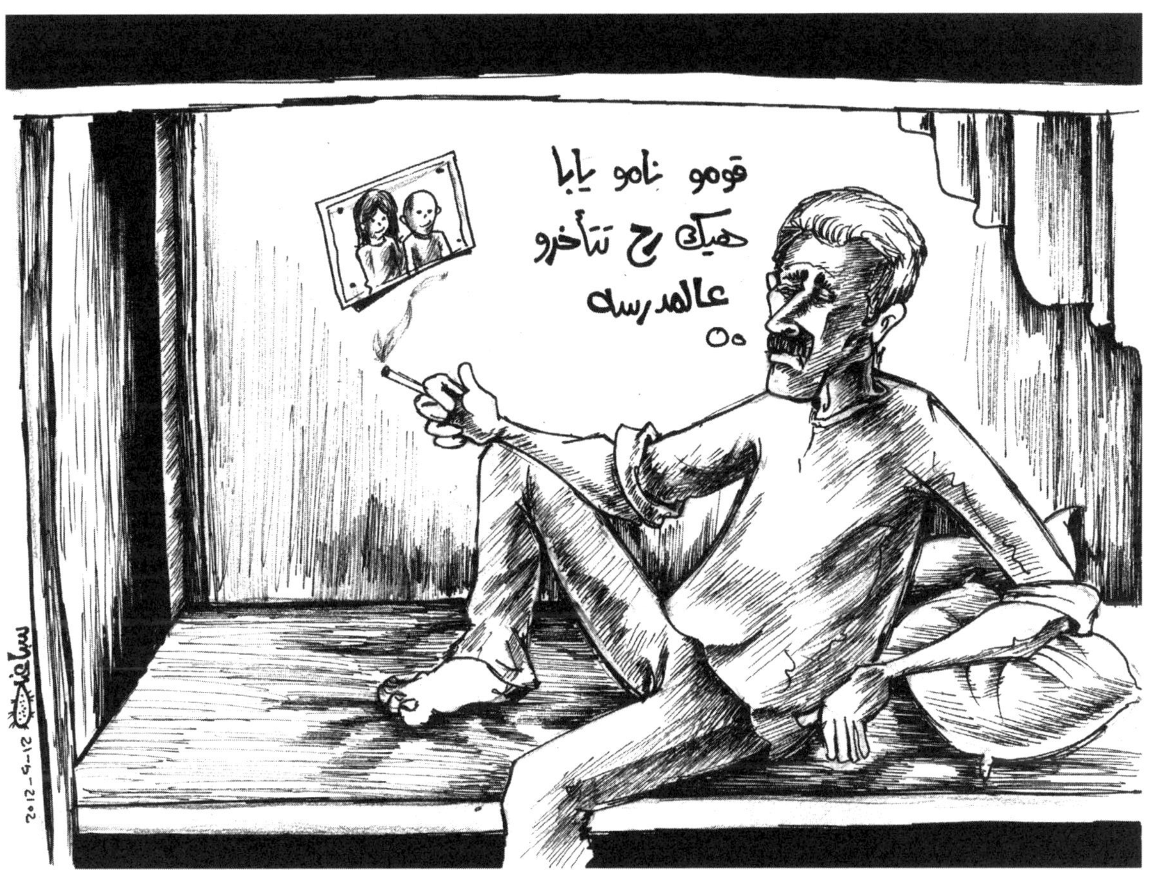

Go to sleep, sweethearts, or you'll be late for school tomorrow.

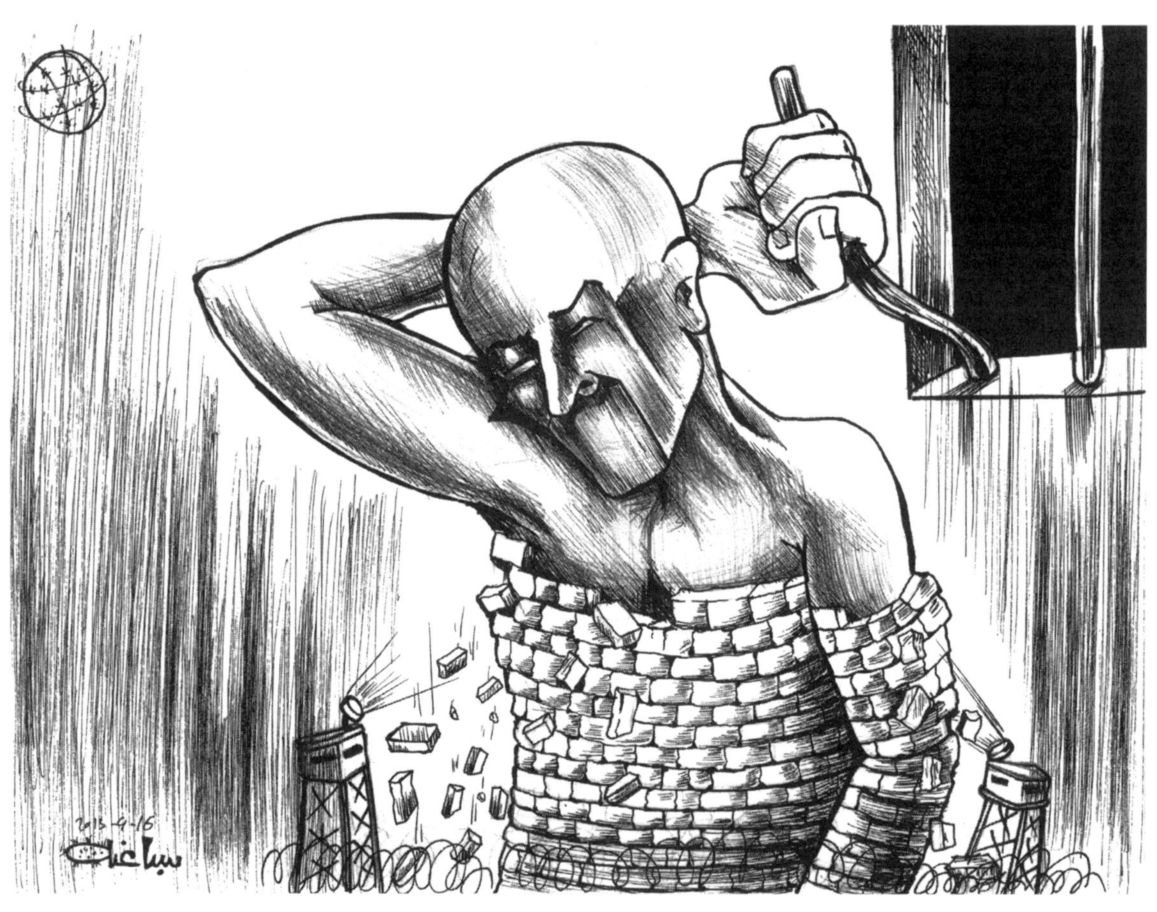

I won't become an object.

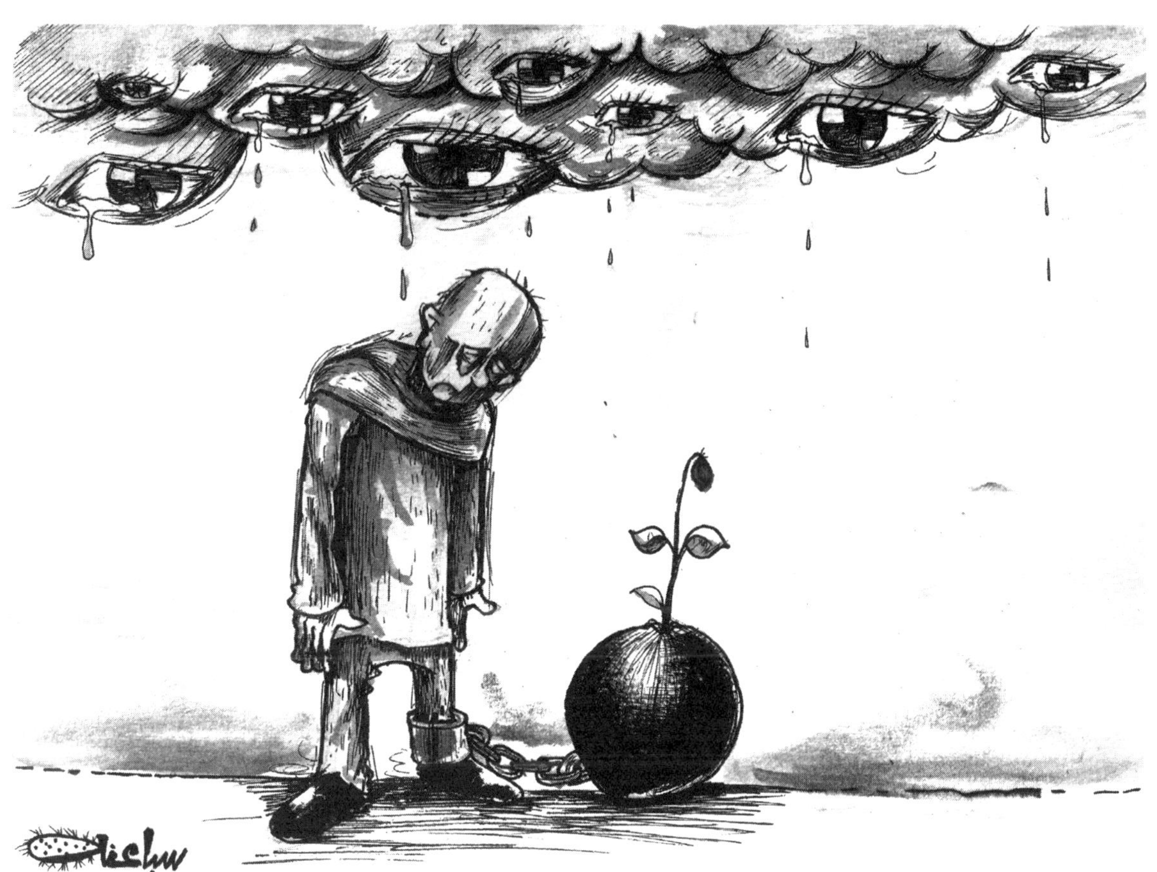

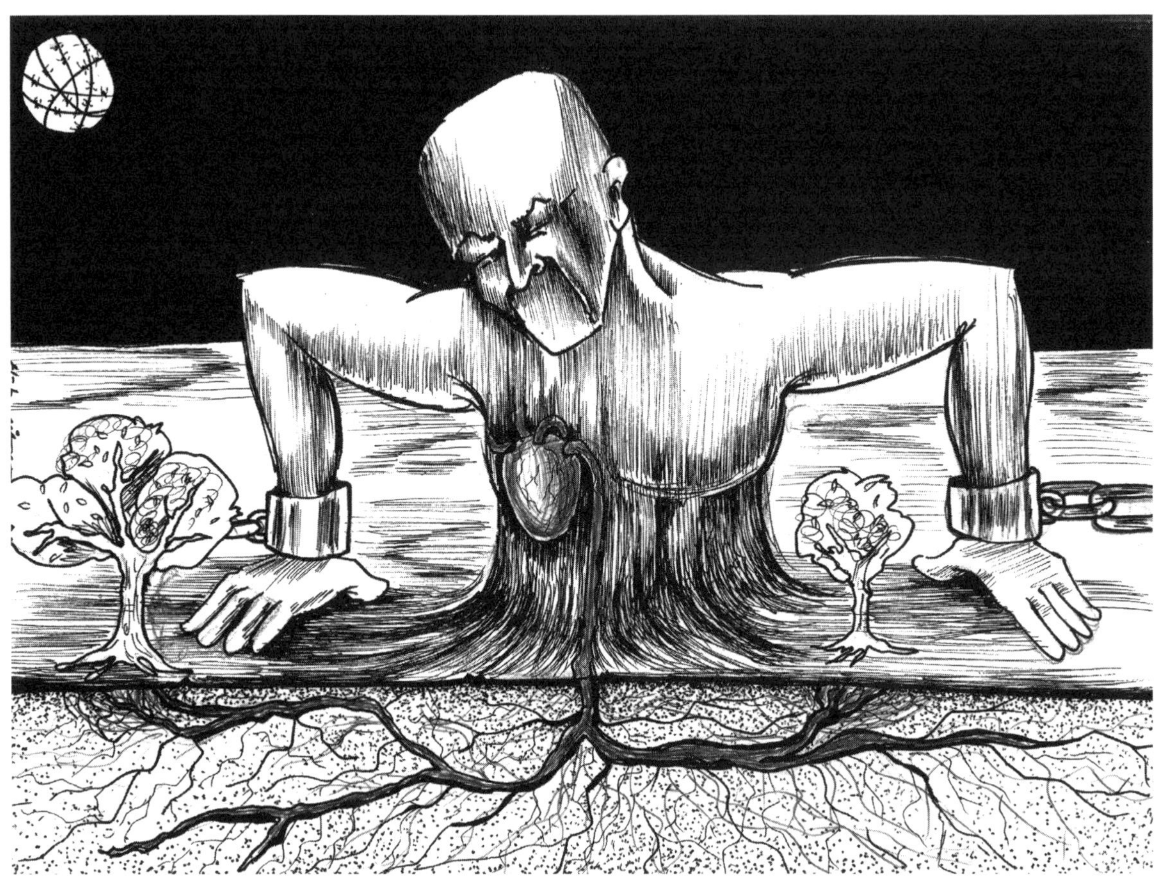

KEY TO SYMBOLS

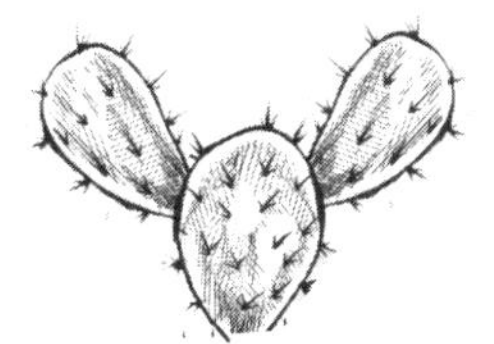

The cactus is used in Palestinian art as a symbol of defiance and *sumud* (steadfastness).

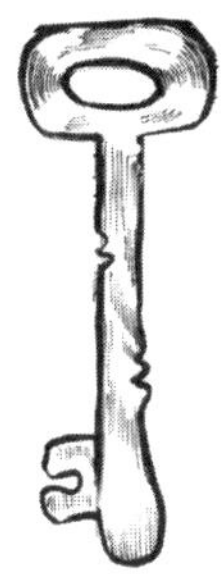

The key symbolises the Palestinians' Right of Return to the homes they were ethnically cleansed from in 1947–48. Refugees took the keys to their homes with them as they fled, expecting to return when hostilities ended. The Right to Return is enshrined in the Universal Declaration of Human Rights.

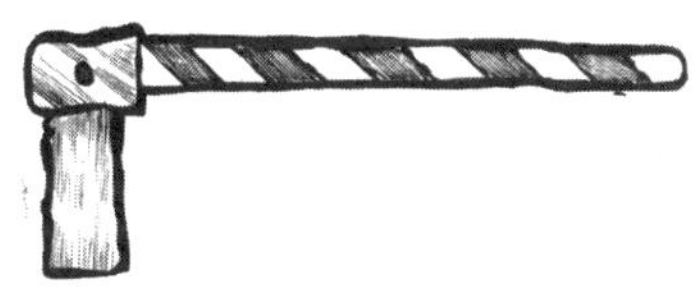

Checkpoints make it difficult for Palestinians to travel even trivial distances without showing identification papers to heavily armed Israeli soldiers or settlers (and sometimes being denied passage altogether).

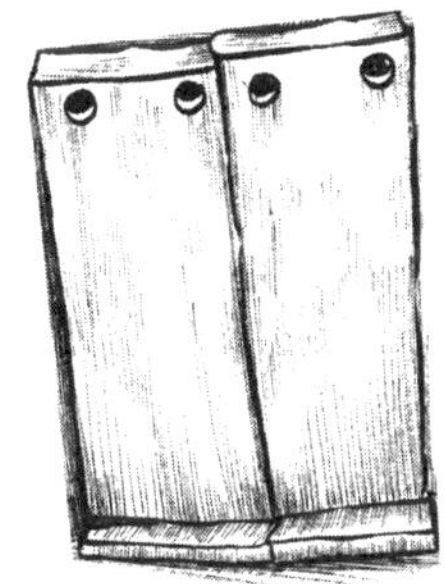

The Apartheid Wall (part of a system that includes barbed wire fencing, watchtowers and sand patrol roads) snakes deep into the West Bank, cutting it into small, easy-to-control segments. In urban areas and elsewhere, the Wall is 25 feet high, 3 times higher than the old Berlin Wall.

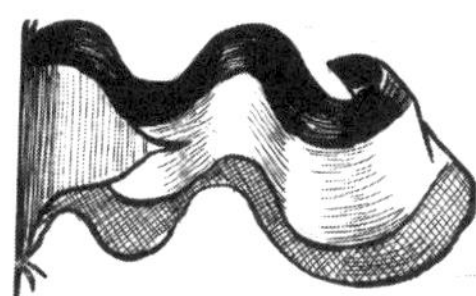

The Palestinian flag is a symbol for the Palestinian people. Prior to the establishment of the Palestinian Authority, raising the Palestinian flag or using the four colours of the flag in combination (in artwork, for example) was cause for arrest by the Israeli occupation authorities.

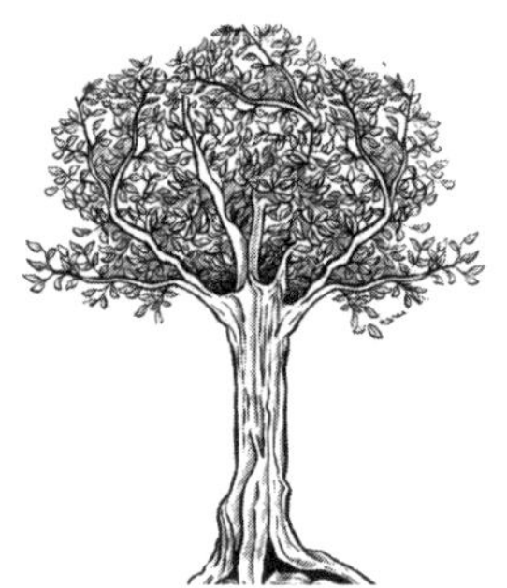

Olive trees have great economic and symbolic significance for Palestinians. Olive trees provide the main source of income for about 80,000 Palestinian families. Israeli soldiers and settlers have uprooted more than 800,000 olive trees since 1967.

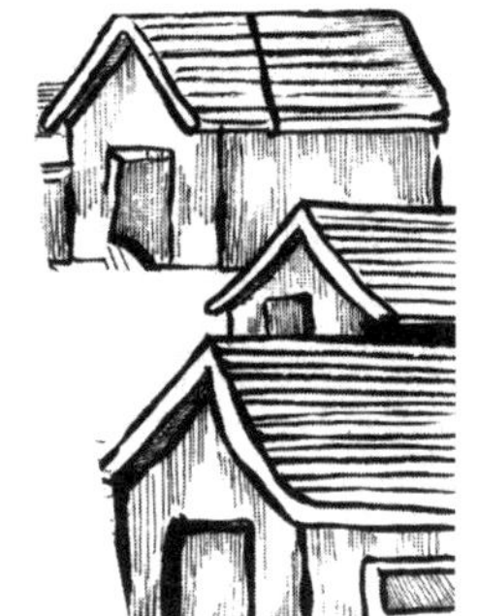

A house in an Israeli settlement, built in the West Bank in contravention of the Fourth Geneva Convention. Many settlements are sited on hilltops above Palestinian towns; often settlers terrorise Palestinian neighbourhoods and the Israeli army does not intervene.

ABOUT THE AUTHOR

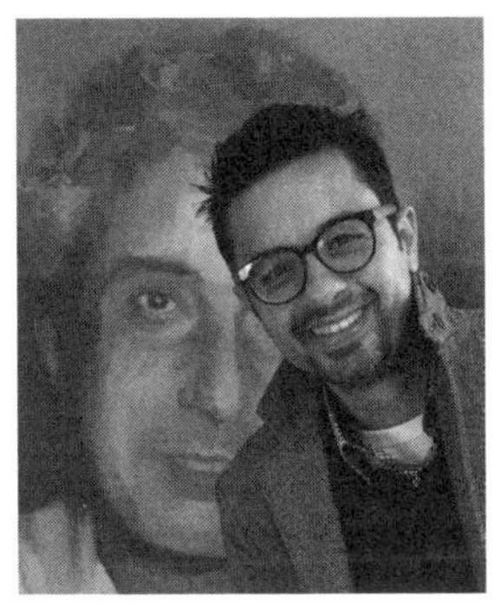

Born in 1979, Mohammad Sabaaneh is a Palestinian painter and caricaturist. He has a daily cartoon in the Palestinian newspaper *al-Hayat al-Jadida* and his work is published in publications across the Arab world. Through the art of caricature, Sabaaneh has worked with deaf students to help them express themselves, and with children who have witnessed Israeli assaults to enable them to process their trauma. He lectures regularly about the art of caricature, including at An-Najah University (West Bank), the New School and School of Visual Arts (New York), and institutions in Spain and Great Britain. Sabaaneh is the Middle East representative for Cartoonist Rights Network International and the Palestinian ambassador for United Sketches, an international association for freedom of expression and cartoonists in exile. His work has been exhibited in solo and group shows around the world. Sabaaneh is the recipient of numerous awards, including the 2017 Marseille International Cartoon Festival Prix d'Or. He lives in Ramallah, Palestine.